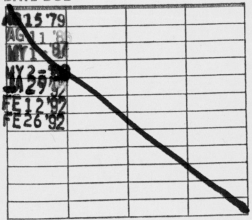

EVERY
SECOND
YEAR

CHARLES O. JONES

EVERY
SECOND
YEAR

Congressional Behavior and the Two-Year Term

THE BROOKINGS INSTITUTION
Washington, D.C.

© *1967 by*
THE BROOKINGS INSTITUTION
1775 Massachusetts Avenue, N.W.
Washington, D.C. 20036

Published November 1967
Second printing December 1968
Third printing September 1969
Library of Congress Catalogue Card Number 67-30596
SBN 8157 4711-x (paper)
SBN 8157 4712-8 (cloth)

THE BROOKINGS INSTITUTION is an independent organization devoted to nonpartisan research, education, and publication in economics, government, foreign policy, and the social sciences generally. Its principal purposes are to aid in the development of sound public policies and to promote public understanding of issues of national importance.

The Institution was founded on December 8, 1927, to merge the activities of the Institute for Government Research, founded in 1916, the Institute of Economics, founded in 1922, and the Robert Brookings Graduate School of Economics and Government, founded in 1924.

The general administration of the Institution is the responsibility of a self-perpetuating Board of Trustees. The trustees are likewise charged with maintaining the independence of the staff and fostering the most favorable conditions for creative research and education. The immediate direction of the policies, program, and staff of the Institution is vested in the President, assisted by an advisory council chosen from the staff of the Institution.

In publishing a study, the Institution presents it as a competent treatment of a subject worthy of public consideration. The interpretations and conclusions in such publications are those of the author or authors and do not purport to represent the views of the other staff members, officers, or trustees of the Brookings Institution.

FOREWORD

Congressional reform has been a major topic of discussion among scholars, journalists, and congressmen themselves in recent years. One of the issues most frequently discussed—the length of term for members of the House of Representatives—is analyzed in this monograph by Charles O. Jones, Professor of Government at the University of Arizona.

Professor Jones, a close student of Congress and the author of books and articles on the legislative process and political parties, examines in detail the recurring debate over the length of term, analyzes the alternatives to the present two-year term, and assesses the prospects for change. He considers the effects of the two-year term on House members, the problems associated with it, possible remedies short of a constitutional amendment, the probability of increasing the length of term in the near future, and the reasons for failure of most efforts to bring about changes. He concludes that the two-year term will be retained for the present, and (despite his initial preference for a four-year term) that it should be retained.

This book is the latest of a number of works on Congress published by Brookings as part of its Governmental Studies program. Titles already published include: *The Congressman*, by Charles

L. Clapp (1963); *Congressional Districting,* by Andrew Hacker (1963; revised in 1964); and *Congressional Control of Administration,* by Joseph P. Harris (1964).

The author draws frequently on the views of numerous congressmen and members of their staffs. The Institution joins him in acknowledging with particular gratitude the help of the congressmen and congressional staff members who attended three round-table discussions at Brookings on the length-of-term question in 1966. Eight Republican congressmen attended the first discussion, held on June 29: James C. Cleveland (New Hampshire), Thomas B. Curtis (Missouri), Charles S. Gubser (California), Jack Edwards (Alabama), Robert McClory (Illinois), Charles A. Mosher (Ohio), Donald Rumsfeld (Illinois), and William B. Widnall (New Jersey). Ten Democratic congressmen attended the second, held on July 12: Jack Brooks (Texas), Robert N. Giaimo (Connecticut), Martha W. Griffiths (Michigan), Donald J. Irwin (Connecticut), William S. Moorhead (Pennsylvania), Abraham J. Multer (New York), Henry S. Reuss (Wisconsin), William F. Ryan (New York), B. F. Sisk (California), and Sidney R. Yates (Illinois). Twelve congressional staff members, five Republicans and seven Democrats, attended the third discussion held on July 14. The Republicans were Warren Butler (Widnall of New Jersey), William T. Kendall (Frelinghuysen of New Jersey), Vincent L. Monzel (Broyhill of North Carolina), Donald W. Olson (Nelson of Minnesota), and Richard Wilbur (minority staff of the Committee on Ways and Means); the Democrats were Dwight H. Barnes (Johnson of California), John R. Buckley (Fascell of Florida), W. Wyche Fowler (Weltner of Georgia), John Morgan (Democratic Study Group), Donald L. Robinson (Reuss of Wisconsin), Mark E. Talisman (Vanik of Ohio), and Fred W. Wegner, Jr. (Brademas of Indiana). The comments of the participating congressmen and staff members are quoted in this book without attribution.

The author also acknowledges gratefully the generous assistance received from George A. Graham, Director of Governmental Studies at Brookings, and from F. P. Kilpatrick, Randall B. Ripley, and James L. Sundquist of the Brookings Senior Staff, all of whom read early drafts of the manuscript. Others who read the manuscript and offered valuable criticism and suggestions were Joseph Cooper, Harvard University; Paul T. David, University of Virginia; Milton C. Cummings, Jr., The Johns Hopkins University; John F. Manley, University of Wisconsin; Samuel C. Patterson, University of Iowa; and Henry H. Wilson, The White House Office. The author thanks Jessica Danson of the University of Arizona for diligently compiling some of the historical data; Imogene Anderson, Janet Hershfield, Karen Ho, and Jeanne Walker of Brookings for efficiently performing a variety of secretarial duties; and James Irish of Tucson for other assistance. The manuscript was capably edited by Richard G. Axt; Florence Robinson prepared the index.

The views expressed in this work are those of the author, and do not necessarily represent the views of the staff members, officers, or trustees of the Brookings Institution.

KERMIT GORDON
President

July 1967
Washington, D.C.

ι

CONTENTS

Contents

CHAPTER
ONE

~~~~~~~

THE TWO-YEAR
COMPROMISE

On January 12, 1966, President Lyndon B. Johnson addressed a joint session of Congress on the State of the Union and proposed a significant constitutional change for the House of Representatives:

> I will ask you to make it possible for Members of the House of Representatives to work more effectively in the service of the Nation through a constitutional amendment *extending the term of a Congressman to 4 years concurrent with that of the President.*

The statement received loud and long applause from the members. Later in his message, the President elaborated on the matter of effectiveness. The present two-year term, he said, "requires most Members of Congress to divert enormous energies to an almost constant process of campaigning, depriving this Nation of the fullest measure of both their skill and their wisdom. Today, too, the work of Government is far more complex than in our early years, requiring more time to learn and more time to master the technical tasks of legislating. And a longer term will serve to attract more men of the highest quality to political life."[1]

1. *Congressional Record* (daily ed.), 89 Cong., 2 sess., Jan. 12, 1966, pp. 130–31, emphasis added.

The proposal, when presented to the 89th Congress, was not a new one. Indeed, it has been one of the more frequent suggestions for reform of the House of Representatives. What was new in 1966 was support from a strong president with a large majority in Congress. Given these circumstances, plus public opinion polls and polls of congressmen indicating broad support, immediate favorable reaction on the Hill and in the press might have been expected.

The very likelihood of effecting the change, however, soon led to second thoughts among congressmen who had indicated support in the past, for a reform they had perhaps thought unlikely to succeed. Similarly, there was somewhat more serious discussion among students of Congress about the probable effects of such a change.

President Johnson emphasized effectiveness of congressmen "in the service of the Nation" when suggesting the four-year term. But what is a congressman doing when he is being "effective?" Or, *What is the proper function of a representative in the House of Representatives and how best may this function be performed?* President Johnson provided one answer to this question in his special message to Congress of January 20, 1966, on the four-year-term proposal. But there are other answers. It is one of those basic questions on which honorable men can disagree.

The current debate over the length of term of members of the House is actually a debate over policy outcomes, public problem solving, and theories of representation. In short, as with all debates over how government should be organized, it is a debate over the fundamentals in this constitutional democracy.

This is, then, a case study of reform—why some men want to make a change, why other men oppose it—of the political effects of the two-year term, and of the reasons the object of reform was created in the first place.

Debate in the Federal Convention

Delegates to the first and second Continental Congresses (1774–75) were chosen largely by extra-legal committees of correspondence and thus had no fixed terms of office. Delegates to the first "official" Congress under the Articles of Confederation were appointed annually, "in such manner as the legislature of each State shall direct . . ."[2] In effect, delegates were usually reappointed as a matter of course. There was, however, a limitation on how many years a delegate could serve in a six-year period. On October 14, 1777, the Continental Congress accepted the proposal offered by John Dickinson (Delaware) that "no person shall be capable of being a delegate for more than three years in any term of six years . . ." Edmund C. Burnett, in his classic study of the Continental Congress, noted that "by this measure, Congress effectively inoculated itself with the germ of pernicious anemia."[3] The final draft of the Articles was approved by Congress on November 15, 1777, ratified by all of the states but Maryland during 1778 and 1779, and came into force in 1781.

Thus, the one-year term had considerable support at the Constitutional Convention when it met in the summer of 1787. It was the practice in many state legislatures as well as the Congress under the Articles, and many agreed with Samuel Adams that "where annual elections end, tyranny begins." The convention moved to adopt the Virginia Plan for purposes of discussion in May 1787. The length of term for House members had been left blank in the Virginia Plan.

On June 12, Roger Sherman and Oliver Ellsworth of Connecticut moved to fill the blank with the words "every year," so as "to bring on some question."[4] John Rutledge (South Carolina) proposed a two-year term and Daniel Jenifer (Maryland) proposed a three-year term. (Table 1 summarizes the sequence of events at the convention relating to the length of term for House members.) As reported in James Madison's notes, the debate

---

2. Articles of Confederation, Art. V.

3. Edmund C. Burnett, *The Continental Congress* (Macmillan, 1941), p. 250. There was a debate on this provision in 1784, when it came time to begin enforcement. At least three members were prevented from taking their seats in that year because they had served three years. Benjamin Franklin had offered no such limitation in his draft of the Articles. See Burnett, pp. 605–06, 216.

4. James Madison (E. H. Scott, ed.), *Journal of the Federal Convention* (Albert, Scott & Co., 1895), p. 151. Subsequent quotations are cited by date rather than page number.

centered around the one- and three-year alternatives (though it is likely that Rutledge had something to say about the two-year term also). Madison stated the case for three years and Elbridge Gerry (Massachusetts) stated the case for one year. Madison justified the longer term in terms of stability and an implicit theory of representation. "Three years will be necessary, in a government so extensive, for members to form any knowledge of the various interests of the States to which they do not belong, and of which they can know but little from the situation and affairs of their own." Thus, representatives in the lower house should focus on the nation as a whole, rather than merely representing their own state's interests. They should be given time to study interests outside those in their own state. Shorter terms, Madison argued, would not provide this time, since "one year will be almost consumed in preparing for, and traveling to and from the seat of national business."

Gerry based his support of the one-year term on several assumptions. First, the people would not accept longer terms; New Englanders in particular "know of the transition made in England from triennial to septennial elections, and will consider such an innovation here [that is, from annual elections to triennial elections] as the prelude to a like usurpation." Second, annual elections constituted "the only defence of the people against tyranny." Gerry believed that what Madison offered was, in reality, "limited monarchy." In effect, Gerry aligned himself with Roger Sherman's constituency-oriented statement on representation that was made later in the debate. Sherman observed (on June 21) that "Representatives ought to return home and mix with the people. By remaining at the seat of government, they would acquire the habits of the place, which might differ from those of their constituents."

Madison, not impressed with either argument, merely commented (June 12) on Gerry's notion that the people would not accept triennial elections. Since no one can really know the opinions of the people on the matter, "we ought to consider what was right and necessary in itself for the attainment of a proper government." If that is done, the recommendation of the convention will be accepted because "all the most enlightened and respectable citizens will be its advocates." If that is not done, "this influential class of citizens will be turned against the plan, and little support in opposition to them can be gained to it from the unreflecting multitude."

Madison temporarily won the day. The three-year term was accepted by a vote of seven to four. The Committee of the Whole

TABLE 1

Sequence of Action on Length of Term for House Members at the Constitutional Convention, 1787

Date	Action taken
May 29	Randolph introduces Virginia Plan; length of term for House members left blank.
May 31	Consideration of length of term postponed.
June 12	Debate in the Committee of the Whole on length of term for House members. Set at three years by vote of 7 to 4 (New York, New Jersey, Pennsylvania, Delaware, Maryland, Virginia, Georgia, in favor; Massachusetts, Connecticut, North Carolina, South Carolina, opposed).
June 13	Report of the Committee of the Whole completed (including three-year terms for House members).
June 15	Paterson introduces New Jersey Plan; one-year terms for members of Congress.
June 19	Report of the Committee of the Whole to the Convention; debate begun.
June 21	Debate in Convention on length of term for House members. Motion to delete "three years" approved—7 to 3 (Massachusetts, Connecticut, Pennsylvania, South Carolina, Virginia, North Carolina, Georgia, in favor; New York, Delaware, Maryland, opposed; New Jersey, divided). Motion to insert "two years" approved unanimously.
July 26	Referral of all resolutions agreed to in Convention to Committee on Detail (including two-year terms for House members).
August 6	Report of Committee on Detail (including a House chosen "every second year").
September 8	Referral of all resolutions to Committee on Revision.
September 12	Report of Committee on Revision (including two-year terms for House members).
September 17	Final draft agreed to by framers.

Source: Compiled from James Madison (E. H. Scott, ed.), *Journal of the Federal Convention* (Albert, Scott & Co., 1895).

completed its report on June 13, thus approving the three-year term.

Then, on June 15, William Paterson (New Jersey) introduced the major counter-plan to the Virginia Plan offered earlier by Randolph. The New Jersey Plan would have merely modified the Articles—apparently retaining unicameralism with one-year appointments for the delegates. Obviously, a compromise was necessary.

On June 21, Edmund Randolph (Virginia) moved to substitute "two years" for "three years" in the third resolution of the report of the Committee of the Whole. As reported in Madison's *Journal*, the two-year proposal was a true compromise. No one except George Mason (Virginia) actually spoke in favor of it. Randolph and Sherman favored annual elections but would be "content with biennial"—Randolph for the reason of the "extent of the United States" and the problem of travel. Oliver Ellsworth (Connecticut), Caleb Strong (Massachusetts), and James Wilson (Pennsylvania) argued for annual elections. They were "pleasing to the people." John Dickinson (Pennsylvania), Madison, and Alexander Hamilton (New York) continued to support the three-year term. Dickinson suggested a rotation system, with one-third of the membership elected for three-year terms each year. Hamilton added the notion that frequent elections tend "to make the people listless to them; and to facilitate the success of little cabals."

Finally, a motion to strike "three years" was approved seven to three, with one delegation divided. The motion to insert "two years" was then approved unanimously, and the question was settled. It only remained for the Committee on Detail to perfect (on August 6) the phrase that appears in the Constitution today, that House members "shall be chosen *every second year*. . . ."

THE SIX-YEAR TERM FOR SENATORS

The debate on June 25 over length of terms for senators found the framers dividing along very much the same lines. There was general agreement that Senate terms should be longer so as to act as a check on the "democratic branch of the National Legislature." There was considerable fear expressed of what the House of Representatives might do. A "firm" Senate would offer stability—protecting both "the people against their rulers [and] . . . the transient impressions into which they themselves might be led." But how long need the Senate term be to accomplish this end? Three, four, five, six, seven, nine-year terms, and "during good behaviour," were all proposed. On June 12, the Committee on the Whole accepted a seven-year term by a vote of eight to one, with New York and Massachusetts divided (see Table 2).

During the convention debate on the committee's report, a number of alternatives were introduced: Nathaniel Gorham (Massachusetts) suggested a four-year term with one-fourth to be elected each year, Hugh Williamson (North Carolina) suggested a six-year term, George Read (Delaware) proposed terms "during good behaviour," and an unidentified delegate made a motion for five-year terms. None of these suggestions was accepted on June 25, but a motion to delete "seven years" from the report was approved. The following day, June 26, Gorham proposed what was eventually adopted, a six-year term with "one-third of the members to go out every second year." Read proposed a nine-year term with "one third going out triennially." Again, James Madison, and Alexander Hamilton who favored life terms, led the debate in favor of the longer term. They relied on the basically anti-democratic rationale that the Senate must act as a check on future "leveling" developments which would likely be reflected in the House.

In framing a system which we wish to last for ages, we should not lose sight of the changes which ages will produce. An increase of population will of necessity increase the proportion of those who will labor under all the hardships of life, and secretly sigh for a more equal distribution of its blessings. These may in time outnumber those who are placed above the feelings of indigence. According to the equal laws of suffrage, the power will slide into the hands of the former. No agrarian attempts have yet been made in this country; but symptoms of a levelling spirit, as we h ve understood, have sufficiently appeared in a certain quarter, to give notice of the future danger.[5]

5. *Ibid.*, p. 243.

TABLE 2

Sequence of Action on Length of Term for Senators at the Constitutional Convention, 1787

Date	Action taken
May 29	Randolph introduces Virginia Plan; length of term for senators left blank.
May 31	Consideration of length of term postponed.
June 7	Pinckney remarks that the Senate ought to be permanent.
June 12	Debate in the Committee of the Whole on length of term for senators. Set at seven years by vote of 8 to 1 (New Jersey, Pennsylvania, Delaware, Maryland, Virginia, North Carolina, South Carolina, Georgia, in favor; Connecticut, opposed; Massachusetts and New York, divided).
June 13	Report of the Committee of the Whole completed (including seven-year terms for senators).
June 15	Paterson introduces New Jersey Plan; no Senate.
June 18	Hamilton submits resolutions as amendments. Senators to serve "during good behaviour."
June 19	Report of the Committee of the Whole to Convention. Debate begun.
June 25	Debate in Convention on length of term for senators. Motion to delete "seven years" approved—7 to 3 (Massachusetts, Connecticut, New York, New Jersey, North Carolina, South Carolina, Georgia, in favor; Pennsylvania, Delaware, Virginia, opposed; Maryland, divided). Motion to insert "six years" failed—5 to 5 (Connecticut, Pennsylvania, Delaware, Virginia, North Carolina, in favor; Massachusetts, New York, New Jersey, South Carolina, Georgia, opposed; Maryland, divided). Motion to insert "five years" failed—5 to 5 (same as above). Four-year terms and "during good behaviour" also proposed.
June 26	Continuation of debate. Motion to insert "nine years" failed—3 to 8 (Pennsylvania, Delaware, Virginia, in favor; Massachusetts, Connecticut, New York, New Jersey, Maryland, North Carolina, South Carolina, Georgia, opposed). Motion to insert "six years" approved—7 to 4 (Massachusetts, Connecticut, Pennsylvania, Delaware, Maryland, Virginia, North Carolina, in favor; New York, New Jersey, South Carolina, Georgia, opposed).
July 26– September 17	See Table 1 (six-year term included in all drafts).

Source: Compiled from the edition of Madison's journal cited as the source of Table 1.

Read lent his support to this general view and added his version of a "national oriented" theory of representation. ". . . State attachments should be extinguished as much as possible; the Senate should be so constituted as to have the feelings of citizens of the whole." James Wilson (Pennsylvania) also supported the longer term—noting that the Senate would probably be most concerned of the two branches with foreign relations and "ought therefore to be made respectable in the eyes of foreign nations."

Roger Sherman, Elbridge Gerry, and General Charles C. Pinckney (South Carolina) led the debate in favor of shorter terms. General Pinckney (not to be confused with the other Charles Pinckney of South Carolina, who favored life terms) wanted four-year terms so that senators would not forget their state's interests. Sherman argued, as he had for shorter House terms, that "frequent elections are necessary to preserve the good behaviour of rulers." At the same time, however, he understood the need for "steadiness and wisdom" in the system. It was his view that either four- or six-year terms would be sufficient to satisfy both requirements. Gerry warned against "every approach towards monarchy."

The nine-year-term proposal was defeated, three to eight. The six-year-term proposal was then passed, seven to four.

The Federalist Rationale

Since the final determination for both houses was a compromise, and thus was not logically justified by either side, it is instructive to examine the arguments put forth in *The Federalist* to defend each compromise. The two-year House term is defended in *Federalist* Nos. 52 and 53, attributed to either Madison or Hamilton. Basically the argument was that frequent elections are essential as long as they aren't too frequent. The authors demonstrate adeptness in combining the rationales which were offered by both sides at the Convention. First, they argue that frequent elections are a good thing. Borrowing from Sherman and Gerry, they state:

As it is essential to liberty that the government in general should have a common interest with the people, so it is particularly essential that the branch of it under consideration should have an immediate dependence on, and an intimate sympathy with, the people. Frequent elections are unquestionably the only policy by which this dependence and sympathy can be effectually secured.[6]

But how frequent need elections be to accomplish the purposes stated above? The authors review various political systems and conclude that danger comes with long terms, not with those which are shorter. Thus biennial elections offer no dangers to the "liberties of the people."

One might use the same rationale for annual, or even more frequent elections, however. The next order of business was to set forth the Madison-Hamilton justification for longer terms. The fear represented by the observation "that where annual elections end, tyranny begins," is misplaced if applied to the constitutional system devised by the framers. The danger comes in political systems which can be altered by the government alone.

But what necessity can there be of applying this expedient to a government limited, as the federal government will be, by the authority of a paramount Constitution? Or who will pretend that the liberties of the people of America will not be more secure under biennial elections, unalterably fixed by such a Constitution, than those of any other nation would be, where elections were annual, or even more frequent, but subject to alterations by the ordinary power of the government?[7]

The next argument, in *Federalist* No. 53, is so much like that made by Madison at the convention that it points to his authorship of the paper. Competent legislators, it is observed, need more than one year to prepare themselves. "The period of service, ought, therefore, in all such cases, to bear some proportion to the extent of practical knowledge requisite to the due performance of the service." Though the period is one year in most states, "the great theatre of the United States presents a very different scene." Further, having knowledge so as to legislate means more than knowing one's constituency, or how govern-

6. Alexander Hamilton, John Jay, and James Madison, *The Federalist* (Modern Library, 1937), p. 343.
7. *Ibid.*, p. 349.

ment works. It also means "some knowledge of the affairs, and even of the laws, of all the States..."[8]

The problem of travel was also presented. The one-year term would work a hardship on members elected from the more distant states. And finally the authors speculated that in any such assembly, a few members would probably be reelected frequently, possess superior talents, and become "masters of the public business." Frequent elections would probably result in greater turnover of most members, and "the greater the proportion of new members, and the less the information of the bulk of the members, the more apt will they be to fall into the snares that may be laid for them" by the few who are always reelected. In conclusion:

> All these considerations taken together warrant us in affirming, that biennial elections will be as useful to the affairs of the public, as we have seen that they will be safe to the liberty of the people.[9]

The lengthier Senate terms were justified as necessary for accomplishing the purposes of the Senate. The second chamber is to provide stability, thoroughness, knowledge, careful consideration of legislation, and attentiveness to the national interest. These goals cannot be achieved by providing another set of legislators elected by the people for short terms. In brief, Madison and Hamilton seemed to be saying, "the people can be trusted, but just in case we are wrong, as we think we probably are, it is best to have some aristocrats around."

What of the problem of the Senate becoming a "tyrannical aristocracy?" If the Senate were itself unchecked, there might be a danger. But the Senate must corrupt a number of related institutions before a major threat exists:

> Before such a revolution can be effected, the Senate, it is to be observed, must in the first place corrupt itself; must next corrupt the State legislatures; must then corrupt the House of Representatives; and must finally corrupt the people at large. It is evident that the Senate must be first corrupted before it can attempt an establishment of tyranny. Without corrupting the State legislatures, it cannot prosecute the attempt, because the periodical change of members would otherwise regenerate the whole body. Without exerting the means of

8. *Ibid.*, pp. 349–50.
9. *Ibid.*, p. 352–53.

corruption with equal success on the House of Representatives, the opposition of that co-equal branch of the government would inevitably defeat the attempt; and without corrupting the people themselves, a succession of new representatives would speedily restore all things to their pristine order.[10]

This is an interesting theory of checks and balances. For present purposes, its interest lies less in whether it is valid than in its use by Madison and Hamilton to justify long terms for senators. The existence of shorter terms and popular election for House members, it seems, permitted the creation of an aristocratic Senate. If the Senate gets "corrupted," the people will express themselves, in part, through the House of Representatives.

Debate in the State Ratifying Conventions

If the records of debates in the state ratifying conventions are reasonably accurate, the length of term for House members was not the subject of extensive debate in any state except Massachusetts. The six-year term for senators was much more frequently discussed. When the House term was discussed, there seemed to be general support for biennial elections, indicating that the compromisers in Philadelphia had done their job well.

At the Massachusetts convention, the most eloquent argument for the logic of a two-year term was set forth by Fisher Ames. He concluded that biennial elections represented a happy medium between two important principles:

A right principle, carried to an extreme, becomes useless. It is apparent that a declaration for a very short term, as for a single day, would defeat the design of representation. The election, in that case, would not seem to the people to be of any importance, and the person elected would think as lightly of his appointment. The other extreme is equally to be avoided. An election for a very long term of years, or for life, would remove the member too far from the control of the people, would be dangerous to liberty, and in fact repugnant to the purposes of the delegation. The truth, as usual, is placed somewhere between the extremes, and I believe is included in this proposition: The term of election must be so long, that the representative may

10. *Ibid.*, pp. 413–14.

understand the interest of the people, and yet so limited, that his fidelity may be secured by a dependence upon their approbation.[11]

Biennial elections fit these criteria, in Ames's judgment. Why weren't annual elections just as good?

At least two years in office will be necessary to enable a man to judge of the trade and interests of the state which he never saw. The time, I hope, will come, when this excellent country will furnish food, and freedom . . . for fifty millions of happy people. Will any man say that the national business can be understood in one year?[12]

Why weren't longer terms—like those of the Senate—just as good? Ames's response to this question is partially revealed in his justification for six-year Senate terms. Senators ". . . are in the quality of ambassadors of the states. . . ." They shouldn't be so close to the people since ". . . then they will represent the state legislatures less, and become the representatives of individuals. *This belongs to the other house.*"[13] Thus, shorter terms bring the representative closer to the people, and that is as it should be for the House of Representatives.

Of those speaking on the question, only Dr. Taylor refused to concede the acceptability of the two-year compromise. To him, it was essential that elections be held annually:

Annual elections have been the practice of this state ever since its settlement, and no objection to such a mode of electing has ever been made. It has, indeed, sir, been considered as the safeguard of the liberties of the people: and the annihilation of it, the avenue through which tyranny will enter. . . . the further we deviate therefrom, the greater the evil.[14]

With the ratification of the Constitution by the required ninth state, New Hampshire, on June 21, 1788, the die was cast. Two-year terms for representatives and six-year terms for senators became institutional characteristics which have persisted to this

---

11. Jonathan Eliot (ed.), *Eliot's Debates*, 5 vols. (Lippincott, 1836), Vol. 2, pp. 7–8. Biennial elections also received brief mention at the North Carolina convention. See Eliot, Vol. 4, pp. 28–29.
12. *Ibid.*, p. 10.
13. *Ibid.*, p. 46, emphasis added.
14. *Ibid.*, p. 5.

day. The debate over length of term represented different views of the function of the two bodies, but terms of various lengths could have been justified by the arguments on both sides. Once set, however, the length of term became one of the institutional characteristics that determine the behavior of those who would serve in Congress. Members of the House would pattern their behavior to accommodate the two-year term. Any change in this institutional characteristic could, therefore, be expected to change much more than just the length of the term.

The Continuing Debate: 1885–1965

Since the ratification of the Constitution, there have been a great many resolutions introduced in Congress to increase the length of term for House members—at least 123 since 1885. Most proposals have been for four years although three-year and six-year terms were suggested in early congresses. But as indicated in Table 3, only three of these proposals (all four-year terms) have emerged from committee and, as nearly as can be determined, hearings directly on the subject of House terms have been very infrequent (certainly fewer than five times since 1885).[15]

Since 1885, the only occasion for House debate on lengthening House terms was in 1906 during the 59th Congress. George W. Norris (R-Nebraska) was successful in committee in attaching his four-year-term proposal to the resolution providing for direct election of senators (House Joint Resolution 120). (Norris was anxious to have his four-year-term proposal attached to the resolution because the direct election of senators was generally favored in both houses. Indeed, it finally did pass in 1913, during the 63rd Congress.) Section 2 of the resolution read: "The term of office of Members of the House of Representatives shall be four years." There was no provision about when the term would begin, although it was apparently assumed that representatives would be elected with the President.

15. In fact, the only extensive hearings held on the subject were in 1965–66, during the 89th Congress.

TABLE 3

Proposals to Change the Length of Term
of House Members, 1885–1966

Length of term	Number of resolutions filed	Reported from committee	Debated	Vote taken
Three years	7	—	—	—
Four years	91	3	1	1
Six years	3	—	—	—
Unspecified	22	—	—	—

Source: Compiled from data collected by Miss Jessica Danson, University of Arizona.

In the committee report, Norris put forward a typically strong argument in favor of four-year terms. The four-year-term proposal is "practically a new question," Norris observed, "although the injustice both to the Member and to the country in general on account of this short term has long been recognized." His first reason for lengthening the term was that though members were elected in November, they did not actually begin their service until December of the following year. "Their term of office has practically half expired before they take the oath. Before they are fairly started in the work for which they were elected they are plunged into a campaign for renomination."[16] That particular problem was resolved with the adoption of the Twentieth Amendment in 1933, which fixed the beginning of the term for the January after election.

The remainder of Norris' argument reads very much like that which is used today to justify the four-year term. First, the members need more time to devote to "solving national legislative problems." Second, political parties should have a chance to test those "policies and principles" for which they stood during the election. The present system may well result in the party being "dethroned" prematurely. Third, certain able legislators "are

16. U. S. Cong., House, Committee on Election of President, Vice-President, and Representatives in Congress, "Election and Term of Office of Members of Congress," Report No. 3165, 59 Cong., 1 sess., April 11, 1906, p. 2.

continually withdrawing from the work" because of the expenses connected with primaries, conventions, campaigns, and elections. Fourth, "men of great ability and honor often refuse to become candidates . . . because they know that before they become familiar with the duties of their office they will be compelled to again enter the arena of political controversy to retain it." Fifth, there is general adverse economic effect from short terms, according to Norris. The congressional election (presumably the mid-term election) "always has a depressing and unhealthy effect upon all branches of business, and there is always during such campaigns and elections an uncertainty in business affairs throughout the country and a hesitancy on the part of business men in the extension and enlargement of their investments." Sixth, "Political grafters" thrive on the short term due to the "partisan strife and . . . the nervous uncertainty controlling candidates . . ." And finally, the voters are "tired of and disgusted with the continual political quarrel and strife." In short, there are just too many elections for the good of the system.[17]

House Joint Resolution 120 was debated on the House floor on June 20, 1906, and much of the time was spent on the four-year-term proposal. Several members objected strongly to combining the Senate and House proposals in one resolution to be voted up or down. William W. Rucker (D-Missouri) asked for unanimous consent to vote on each section separately, but objections were heard.[18]

Other members attacked the four-year term in and of itself. Oscar W. Gillespie (D-Texas) offered some free advice to the American voter—"Hold the Whip hand over your Member of Congress. [Loud Applause]" William T. Tyndall (R-Missouri) observed that Congress ought to be close to the people. "I will say that it might not be a bad thing if this Congress were cleaned

---

17. *Ibid.,* pp. 2–3.

18. David A. DeArmond (D-Missouri), for example, favored the direct election of senators, "But now we have it, through the wisdom of the committee, through the perverseness of the committee, through the honesty but bad judgment of the committee, or through deceptive purposes—we have the proposition so coupled that the one is to be weighted and loaded down by the other." DeArmond referred to it as "a new and strange proposition." *Congressional Record,* 59 Cong., 1 sess., June 20, 1906, p. 8830.

out oftener than it really is. [Laughter and Applause]" Horace O. Young (R-Michigan) asked whether the logic of the four-year-term proposal wasn't that "we should adopt a monarchy and not have any election?"[19]

Only William B. Cockran (D-New York) supported Norris.

This whole service . . . is confined to two sessions. In the first everything tends to make him incapable, and in the second to make him indifferent. We declare at every stage that the House is declining in influence. Yet we lose no chance to push it farther along the downward slope.[20]

The results, according to Cockran, were that the other institutions, notably the Senate, gained in influence at the expense of the House.

Following the debate, a division vote was taken. The result was 89 in favor, 86 opposed. Thus, the resolution failed to get the two-thirds majority necessary for constitutional amendments. Interest in extending the term to four years did not, however, disappear with this vote. A total of twenty-five resolutions were introduced in the next eight Congresses (60th to 67th).

The next major attempt to extend the term came in 1923, when the Committee on Elections again reported a resolution for a four-year term. The argument in favor of the resolution, as recorded in the committee report, is particularly interesting since it was based almost entirely on the need to provide more support for the President. This argument had not been relied on to any great extent to that date (certainly not at the Constitutional Convention), nor has it been relied on since by very many proponents of the four-year term because it is not a particularly popular view with members of Congress. But in this 1923 committee report, the Republican majority put the case bluntly:

A majority of the Members of the House of Representatives elected when a President is elected, is usually of the same political faith as the President. That is as it should be. To tie his hands by the election of a majority of different political faith at the middle of his term seems most unwise. If allowed to work out his own plans and purposes for

19. *Ibid.*, pp. 8829–31.
20. *Ibid.*, p. 8831.

the full term, he may accomplish great things, but surely can do little if he is handicapped by a Congress that will not support him.[21]

No other new arguments were presented, but one striking *non sequitur* is worth quoting: "Surely any man who is worthy of being elected for two years is worthy of being intrusted with the position for four years."[22]

The 1923 resolution was not debated during the 67th Congress. Since that time no similar resolution has been reported from a committee, though on February 24, 1931, an unsuccessful attempt was made to amend the Twentieth Amendment, then being debated in the House, so as to provide four-year terms for House members.[23] Until 1965, the only activity concerning the four-year term, aside from the annual introduction of resolutions, occurred in the 79th and 83rd Congresses. Some references were made to extending House terms during the hearings before the Joint Committee on the Organization of Congress in 1945 (two members suggested six-year terms), but the Committee did not recommend any changes.[24] Hearings were held for one day during the 83rd Congress but no further action was taken.

Summary

The length of term for House members was set at two years because that was an acceptable compromise for most of those favoring either one- or three-year terms. It was rationalized before the

21. U. S. Cong., House, Committee on Election of President, Vice-President and Representatives in Congress, "Electing Representatives in Congress for Term of Four Years," Report No. 1613, 67 Cong., 4 sess., Feb. 15, 1923, p. 1.

22. *Loc. cit.*

23. William B. Bankhead (D-Alabama) introduced the amendment which read in part as follows: ". . . the terms of Representatives [shall end] at noon on the 4th day of January two years after such terms would have ended if this article had not been ratified; and the terms of their successors shall then begin." A point of order that the Bankhead amendment was not germane was upheld by the Chairman of the Committee on the Whole and his ruling was sustained by a vote of the membership, 147 to 76. Thus, Bankhead's clever proposal was never debated. See *Congressional Record*, 72 Cong., 3 sess., Feb. 24, 1931, p. 5900.

24. U. S. Cong., Joint Committee on the Organization of Congress, Hearings, "Organization of Congress," 79 Cong., 1 sess., 1945, pp. 333, 1081.

public and state ratifying conventions on that basis. Because it was a compromise between those who wanted shorter terms and those who wanted longer terms, both sides in the current discussion over length of term can, and do, find support for their positions in those early debates.

No Congress has shown any great anxiety to experiment with the length of term for House members. As Nelson W. Polsby and Robert L. Peabody have so clearly pointed out, there are many unpredictable consequences from changes of this type.[25] The proposed four-year term is not a reform like that of the direct election of senators (merely institutionalizing a practice which had already gained wide acceptance) or like that of reorganizing the committee system (a change with considerable support, to make the House more efficient). Changing the length of terms of House members may have many desirable consequences or many undesirable consequences, thus making the reform rather risky. Or it may result in very little change at all, thus making the reform unnecessary. It is the purpose of the remainder of this study to present the various dimensions of the debate, to analyze the effects of the two-year term, and to speculate about the prospects and consequences of change.

25. Robert L. Peabody, "Rebuild the House?" *The Johns Hopkins Magazine,* Vol. 17 (March, 1966), pp. 8–11, 21–22; Nelson W. Polsby, "The President's Modest Proposal," *Public Administration Review,* Vol. 26 (Sept., 1966), pp. 156–59.

CHAPTER
TWO

~

PROPOSALS FOR
A FOUR-YEAR TERM

No institution which must depend upon itself for reform can be expected to be the subject of reform very often. Special conditions must exist before congressmen are willing to upset long-established processes to which they have grown accustomed. Many would argue that one source of strength for Congress is its stability and that too many changes, too often, would be detrimental to congressional strength. Given this analysis, the most likely condition for congressional reform would be when members have convinced themselves that existing processes are resulting in a loss of congressional strength and effectiveness. Such seemed to be the case in 1945 and 1946, when Congress passed the only broad reform legislation in its history. Having just experienced the Depression and World War II, and having witnessed the tremendous increase in the power of the executive in relation to themselves, congressmen were prepared to act. They even went so far as to eliminate a large number of committees, all of which had chairmen and ranking minority members.

Congress continues to be concerned about its strength and effectiveness relative to the executive. In response to a considerable outpouring of criticism from journalists, scholars, and congressmen themselves, Congress in 1965 established another Joint Committee on the Organization of Congress.[1] The committee was charged to "make a full and complete study of the organization and operation of the Congress . . . and . . . recommend improvements in such organization and operation . . ."[2] The committee was composed of six members from each house, with equal representation from the two parties. Senator Mike Monroney (D-Oklahoma), a member of the 1945 Joint Committee, and Representative Ray J. Madden (D-Indiana) served as co-chairmen.

Congressional Interest Revives

The joint committee began its hearings in May 1965. It was to be expected that one of the more frequently mentioned reforms during the hearings would be that of extending House terms to four years. Several witnesses discussed this reform, and Co-chairman Madden frequently asked for opinions from those who failed to mention it. As Madden noted in his opening remarks to the hearings:

> When a Member is sworn into office in January, after his November election, he is then within 12 months of another campaign and a great deal of his time and money is spent on and wasted in an almost around-the-clock campaign for reelection under the 2-year term provision.[3]

In addition to the attention it received before the joint committee, the four-year term proposal was examined before Subcommittee No. 5 of the House Committee on the Judiciary and the Subcommittee on Constitutional Amendments of the Senate Committee on the Judiciary. Hearings were held in the House

1. For a sample of some of this criticism see the *Congressional Record* (daily ed.), 88 Cong., 2 sess., Jan. 22, 1964, pp. 520–50. See also James M. Burns, *The Deadlock of Democracy: Four-Party Politics in America* (Prentice-Hall, 1963); and Joseph S. Clark, *Congress: The Sapless Branch* (Harper and Row, 1964) and *The Senate Establishment* (Hill and Wang, 1963).

2. U. S. Cong., Sen. Con. Res. 2, 89 Cong., 1 sess. (1965).

3. U. S. Cong., Joint Committee on the Organization of the Congress, Hearings, "Organization of Congress," 89 Cong., 1 sess. (1965) Pt. 1, p. 6.

committee August 18–26, 1965, and again in February and
March in 1966. Senate hearings were held July 13–14, 1966. (As
noted earlier, this was apparently only the third time the proposal had been the subject of congressional hearings since 1885.)
The 1965 House hearings evidenced widespread support for the
four-year-term proposal. Of the sixty-seven congressmen who
testified or submitted statements, sixty-five favored some form of
the four-year term; only one (Herbert Tenzer, D-New York) favored a three-year term, and only one (Edward J. Derwinski,
R-Illinois) opposed lengthening the term.

There were earlier indications of support for a four-year term.
Representative Abraham J. Multer (D-New York) had conducted
a poll of the House membership in 1949 to determine support
for his resolution proposing the four-year term. Multer's resolution provided that all members would be elected with the President. The results, as he reported them to the subcommittee in
1965, were 319 members in favor (75 percent) and only 110 opposed.[4]

Representative Frank Chelf (D-Kentucky) has been the most
persistent supporter of the four-year term in the House. Before
reintroducing his resolution in 1965, Chelf polled both House
and Senate members. His resolution called for half of the membership to be elected for four-year terms during presidential election years and half during the mid-term election years. Chelf
received 362 replies in the House; of these, 254 (70 percent of his
replies but only 58 percent of the total membership) were in
favor, 41 opposed, and 67 "remain doubtful." "My poll of the
Senate," Chelf reported, "reveals that two-thirds of that body are
for this bill."[5]

In a general study of congressional reform, Roger H. Davidson, David M. Kovenock, and Michael O'Leary interviewed
eighty House members in 1963. On the question of the four-year
term (all members to be elected in presidential election years),

4. U. S. Cong., House, Committee on the Judiciary, Subcommittee No. 5, "Congressional Tenure of Office," 89 Cong., 1 and 2 sess. (1965–66), p. 29. Cited hereafter
as Subcommittee No. 5, *Hearings*.

5. *Ibid.*, p. 19.

they found that sixty-eight percent were in favor. Only six percent thought that it was likely to be enacted, however.[6]

These are particularly interesting findings in view of what actually happened to the legislation in 1966. A great many congressmen expressed themselves in favor of the change when there was little prospect of its being enacted. When the President announced his support, however, and the proposal actually got on the agenda of Congress, many congressmen apparently had second thoughts. Evidence for this switch is found in a poll conducted by the *Congressional Quarterly* in January 1966, after the President's speech. Members of both houses were asked, "Do you favor a four-year House term?" (No distinction was made among the four-year-term proposals.) Though less than half (251 of 535) of the members responded, the results showed that many members were opposed to extending the term. Fifty-five percent of those who responded were in favor, forty-five percent were opposed. The split was about the same in both houses, but there were differences between the two parties. A large majority of Republicans were opposed and a large majority of Democrats were in favor.[7]

In testimony before both the joint committee and Subcommittee No. 5, congressmen noted that there was support for extending the term to four years among constituents as well as congressmen. Representative Chelf reported that "many of my colleagues . . . have conducted individual polls, and . . . they ranged all the way from 70 to 75, and one instance 80 percent of their people for this legislation."[8]

The Gallup Poll results tended to support these reports. The January 1966 Gallup figures showed the public to be 61 percent in favor, 24 percent opposed, and 15 percent with no opinion,

6. Roger H. Davidson et al., *Congress in Crisis: Politics and Congressional Reform* (Wadsworth, 1966). See also the testimony of Davidson, Kovenock, and O'Leary before the Joint Committee on the Organization of the Congress, Pt. 5, pp. 744–82, and before Subcommittee No. 5 of the House Committee on the Judiciary, pp. 294–300.

7. *Congressional Quarterly Weekly Report*, Feb. 11, 1966, p. 364.

8. Subcommittee No. 5, *Hearings*, p. 20.

when asked about the four-year term.[9] The results show an increase in those favoring the proposal over earlier polls taken in 1961 (51 percent in favor) and 1946 (40 percent in favor).[10]

This apparent broad support in Congress and among the public for the four-year term can be offered as one explanation why the President included it in the State of the Union message. And while delivering the speech, President Johnson surely must have satisfied himself that he was right to include the proposal, since it received loud and long applause from the members. It seemed at that moment that the necessary conditions existed for an important change in the House of Representatives.

President Johnson's Four-Year-Term Proposal

The President's proposal was introduced in the House by Frank Chelf (D-Kentucky) and in the Senate by Birch Bayh (D-Indiana). The resolution (House Joint Resolution 807 and Senate Joint Resolution 126) read as follows:

> *Resolved by the Senate and House of Representatives of the United States of America in Congress assembled (two-thirds of each House concurring therein),* That the following article is proposed as an amendment to the Constitution of the United States, which shall be valid to all intents and purposes as a part of the Constitution when ratified by the legislatures of three-fourths of the several States within seven years from the date of its submission by the Congress:

"ARTICLE _____

"SECTION 1. The terms of Representatives shall be four years and shall commence at noon on the 3d day of January of the year in which the regular term of the President is to begin.

"SEC. 2. No Member of a House of Congress shall be eligible for election as a Member of the other House for a term which is to begin before the expiration of the term of the office held by him unless, at least thirty days prior to such election, he shall have submitted a

9. American Institute of Public Opinion, *Gallup Political Index*, Report No. 8, Jan. 1966, p. 9.

10. "Congressional Reform," *Congressional Quarterly Special Report*, April 1, 1964, p. 49.

resignation from such office which shall become effective no later than the beginning of such term.

"SEC. 3. This article shall take effect on January 3, 1973, if it is ratified prior to January 1, 1972; otherwise, it shall take effect on January 3, 1977."

Two features in particular should be noted about the President's proposal. First, all House members would be serving four-year terms during the same period of time as the President. Presumably this would mean that they would be elected at the same time as the President (although Congress could change the 1845 election law and have House members elected at a different time). Second, the provision requiring a member to resign before seeking election to "the other House" was designed to calm Senate fears. If they had four-year terms, there would be occasions when congressmen would be able to run for the Senate without risk since they would be in the middle of a four-year term. Senators were not anxious to provide House members with a "free crack" at election to the upper chamber.

The principal spokesman for the administration before Subcommittee No. 5 was Attorney General Katzenbach. His statement supplemented the presidential message on the four-year term that was read before the House on January 20, 1966. The argument of the President, Katzenbach, and other supporters of the concurrent-term proposal is summarized in the following sections.[11]

CONDITIONS FOR CHANGE

Four conditions which establish the need for a longer term were noted by proponents of the four-year term.

1. Society is changing and public problems are more complex than ever before. "It is no longer sufficient to develop solutions for an agricultural nation with few foreign responsibilities. . . ." [P]

---

11. The President's message is in the *Congressional Record* (daily ed.), 89 Cong., 2 sess., Jan. 20, 1966, pp. 748–50; quotes in the text are marked [P]. The Attorney General's testimony is in Subcommittee No. 5, *Hearings*, pp. 179–84; quotes in the text are marked [AG].

2. More complex public problems naturally find their way to Congress.

In the First Congress 142 bills were introduced, and 108 public laws enacted. In the 88th Congress, 15,299 bills were introduced and 666 public laws were enacted. . . . Representatives today are faced with a whole spectrum of complex and diverse issues flowing from advanced technology, growing population, and international commitments. They range from the problems of crime to the strategy of nuclear defense. . . . This volume, complexity, and diversity make it difficult even for a veteran Member to be its master. How much are these difficulties magnified for a freshman Congressman—and each Congress has a substantial complement of new Members. [AG]

3. Congressional sessions are longer now.

The competitive pressures imposed by the two-year term, when the incumbent must remain in Washington into the Fall to attend the public business, reduce his capacity to do either task—campaigning or legislating—with the complete attention his conscience and the public interest demand. [P]

4. The costs of living continue to increase, congressional districts increase in population, and new campaign techniques are developed—thus making it increasingly expensive to campaign for office. "Their great and steadily rising costs have priced many worthy candidates out of a political career. The frequency of campaigning severely aggravates the problem." [AG]

ADVANTAGES TO BE GAINED

The four-year term, its proponents argue, will be a direct solution for the conditions stated above. Thus, a number of advantages for the political system will result.

Recruitment. The frustrations and costs of continuous campaigning prevent a number of qualified men from seeking the job. The change will "attract the best men in private and public life into competition for this high public office." [P] Obviously this point had to be handled gingerly by the President so as not to imply that the present membership was unqualified. The implication is clear, however, that the proponents think men of higher quality will be attracted to run for the House if the term is four years.

A complementary advantage would be that men of quality would not leave the house. As Representative Chelf observed about his own voluntary retirement:

> I have had to make four hard, brutal, costly races in the past 3 years, and I cannot stand this. Really and truly I cannot stand it financially to remain on in Congress much longer with such a financial drain.[12]

Elections. There are a number of electoral and campaign advantages which presumably would result from the change. First and foremost, by reducing the number of elections, it is expected that the costs of reelection will go down—perhaps be cut in half. Second, the costs to the states in administering elections would be reduced. Some members predicted a saving of millions of dollars. Third, the four-year term would free the member "from the inexorable pressures of biennial campaigning for reelection." [P] Thus, the mental costs of frequent campaigning would be reduced and the member would increase his effectiveness on the job in Washington. And finally, with all members running with the President, elections for the House of Representatives would focus on national problems instead of local problems. There would be a greater likelihood of offering the public a choice between two party programs, even at the level of congressional races.

Policy Making. The most important advantage for solving public problems would be that the President would have a greater assurance than he now has of majority support in Congress.

The presidential election is the only truly national election, when all the people have the opportunity to install a new administration. Their choice should include the right to elect as Representatives men who they believe will help the President they have selected. [AG]

12. Subcommittee No. 5, *Hearings*, p. 18. Chelf meant the primary and the general elections in 1962 and 1964.

... When we elect a person of one party as President, he ought to have the majority of his party in Congress so that responsibility is on the party, if we believe in the two-party system. ... Divided responsibility should be avoided.[13]

A second advantage is related to one of the electoral advantages. With less campaigning, and less preoccupation with upcoming campaigns, the member will have more time to "bring his best judgment to bear on the great questions of national survival, economic growth, and social welfare." [P] In short, the representative will have more time to legislate. A third policy advantage is that members will be more independent—both of their constituencies and of pressure groups. Since they do not have to seek reelection as often, and need less money for campaigning, there will be a reduction in the "influence of large contributors, pressure groups, and special interest lobbyists." [P] Finally, the four-year term will allow members to face controversial issues. At present, many problems are simply shunted aside every other year because members are concerned about reelection. Brookings round table participants described some of these situations:[14]

CONGRESSMAN A: I think that the four years would help you to be a braver congressman, and I think what you need is bravery. I think you need courage. Most congressmen are quite able to see all the arguments, they understand how a thing is going to work, but they don't understand perfectly whether or not their district is going to take care of this. One of the congressmen came to me who has voted on every civil rights bill and he said, "And I want to vote on the fair housing bill, but I don't have time to explain it to 400,000 people," and you really don't.

CONGRESSMAN B: Could I cite another bill ...? I don't mind naming it. This is the situs picketing bill. Probably most people would be for it. I happen to be for it. ... That bill is not going to come up this year. You know why it is not coming up?

CONGRESSMAN A: It is too hot.

CONGRESSMAN B: Because 435 of us have to face election. It is that simple. It is not because Powell [Chairman Adam Clayton Powell of

13. Subcommittee No. 5, *Hearings*, p. 308.

14. Participants in the Brookings congressional round table are listed in the Foreword. A companion volume, Charles L. Clapp, *The Congressman: His Work as He Sees It* (Brookings Institution, 1963), also draws upon a congressional round table.

the Committee on Education and Labor] doesn't want to call it up.
. . . If we had a four-year term, I am as confident as I can be the bill
would have come to the floor and passed.

General. Since longer terms for congressmen will result in the
advantages noted above, the prestige of Congress will be en-
hanced. The four-year term would "restore to the Congress its
function as a coequal in the three great branches of government."[15]

SUPPORTING ARGUMENTS

A number of supporting arguments are offered by the proponents—some more persuasive than others.

1. Many of the participants at the Constitutional Convention
actually favored longer terms—notably James Madison and Alexander Hamilton. Thus, there is nothing sacred about the two-
year term. It was a compromise, one which is simply no longer
suitable to the needs of the present century.[16]

2. Other public offices have longer terms. Most governors,
other state administrative officials and state senators have four-
year terms, and five states have adopted four-year terms for the
lower house. The trend is clear. Further, in other democratic
countries legislative terms are four years or longer.[17]

3. There is support for the proposal among those who must
pass on it. The Senate favors it. Indeed, Senator Frank E. Moss
(D-Utah) testified that "there will be a two-thirds majority available in the Senate."[18] State legislatures also would probably be
in favor of it—particularly since it would offer ambitious state
legislators a more attractive office to seek. Finally, public opinion
favors four-year terms for congressmen. The Gallup Poll shows
this to be the case. And polls by individual members show public
support. In fact, one member noted that "very few constituents
are aware their representatives serve for only 2 years."[19]

15. Subcommittee No. 5, *Hearings*, p. 107.
16. See *Ibid.*, pp. 66–68, 179–80.
17. *Ibid.*, pp. 213–16; p. 35.
18. *Ibid.*, p. 121.
19. *Ibid.*, p. 73.

4. There has been considerable support for this proposal among political scientists. Attorney General Katzenbach cited the supporting views of several political scientists in his testimony—James M. Burns, Stephen K. Bailey, Herman Finer, Roland Young, and Louis W. Koenig.[20] It is a fact that many prominent political scientists have supported a concurrent-term proposal. The report of the Committee on Political Parties of the American Political Science Association, "Toward a More Responsible Two-Party System," recommended such a change.[21] This recommendation was one of the few which appeared at the time to be noncontroversial.

Other Four-Year-Term Proposals

In discussing the arguments of the proponents of the four-year term, it is necessary to point out that there are three separate four-year-term proposals with fundamental differences. The President's proposal, which was so warmly applauded by the members, provided that the members would all be elected in presidential election years (the *concurrent* term). A second four-year proposal is that half of the members be elected with the President and half during mid-term elections. It was this *staggered* term which received so much favorable testimony during the August 1965 hearings before Subcommittee No. 5. Of the

20. *Ibid.,* pp. 184–86.
21. "Toward a More Responsible Two-Party System," *American Political Science Review,* Vol. 44 (September, 1950), Supplement, p. 75. For other support of this proposal see Stephen K. Bailey, *The Condition of Our National Parties* (Fund for the Republic, 1959); James M. Burns, *The Deadlock of Democracy: Four-Party Politics in America* (Prentice-Hall, 1963); and Herman Finer, *The Presidency: Crisis and Regeneration* (University of Chicago Press, 1960). It should be noted that not all political scientists agree with those cited above. Many support the retention of the two-year term. See Robert L. Peabody, "Rebuild the House?" *The Johns Hopkins Magazine,* Vol. 17 (March, 1966), pp. 8–11, 21–22; and Nelson W. Polsby, "The President's Modest Proposal," *Public Administration Review,* Vol. 26 (September, 1966) pp. 156–59. For a bibliography of views of political scientists and journalists see Dorothy C. Tompkins, *Changes in Congress* (Institute of Governmental Studies, University of California, 1966), pp. 33–39.

sixty-five House members who indicated support for four-year terms in those hearings, only *five* favored running with the President. The rest favored splitting the House. A third proposal is to have all members elected during the mid-term or *off-year* elections, though no such resolution was introduced in the 89th Congress.[22]

Proponents of each proposal set forth the conditions which demand a four-year term, the advantages to be gained from the change, and various supporting arguments for change. While there is considerable agreement about the conditions which create the need for a longer term and about the supporting arguments, there is *disagreement* over the advantages. Those opposed to having all members run with the President, for example, express fears about the independent status of Congress and the traditional "checks and balances."

THE STAGGERED TERM

Most of those who testified in favor of a four-year term before Subcommittee No. 5 supported the proposal which would elect one-half of the members during presidential election years, and one-half during off-year elections. The most popular version of this proposal was introduced in 1965 by Representative Chelf as House Joint Resolution 394. It is somewhat more complicated than the concurrent-term proposal of the President, as can be seen from the text of the resolution on page 32.

There are several features to note about this proposal. Mid-term congressional elections would continue but only one-half of each state delegation would be seeking reelection then. The staggered system would get underway by having the members draw lots to determine who would serve two and who would serve four years. When the decennial reapportionment increased or decreased the size of a state delegation, lots would again be

22. There were other proposals as well. Representative Herbert Tenzer (D-New York) proposed a three-year term; Representative Donald Rumsfeld (R-Illinois) proposed alternating two- and four-year terms. See Subcommittee No. 5, *Hearings,* pp. 37–41, 324–26.

Resolved by the Senate and House of Representatives of the United States of America in Congress assembled (two-thirds of each House concurring therein), That the following article is proposed as an amendment to the Constitution of the United States. . . .

"SECTION 1. The United States House of Representatives shall be composed of Members chosen every second and fourth year by the people of the several States, and the electors in each State shall have the qualifications requisite for electors of the most numerous branch of the State legislature. Except as otherwise provided in this article, the term of office of a Representative shall be four years.

"SEC. 2. Immediately after the convening of the Congress after the first regular election to which this article applies, the Members of the House of Representatives of each State delegation shall assemble and be divided by lot as equally as may be into two classes. The seats of the Members of the first class shall be vacated at the expiration of the second year, and the seats of the Members of the second class shall be vacated at the expiration of the fourth year, so that, as nearly as possible, one-half of the Members of the House of Representatives in the delegation from each State shall be elected every second year.

"SEC. 3. When a number of Representatives of a State are increased or decreased following a reapportionment of Representatives among the several States, all of the Members of the House of Representatives from that State elected at the first election following the reapportionment shall be divided by lot, as equally as may be, into two classes as provided in section 2 of this article, so that, as nearly as possible, the seats of the Members of the first class shall be vacated at the expiration of the second year, and the seats of the Members of the second class shall be vacated at the expiration of the fourth year, and, as nearly as possible, one-half of the Members from that State shall be elected every two years. When a vacancy occurs by resignation of a Member of the House of Representatives, or otherwise, the Member elected to fill that vacancy shall serve for the unexpired period of the term of the Member originally elected for that House seat.

"SEC. 4. A Member of the House of Representatives shall not seek or accept the nomination or election to any elective office other than that of United States Representative during his term of office, except when a vacancy occurs in another elective office during his term. Otherwise, a Representative shall submit his resignation as a Member of the House of Representatives prior to seeking or accepting the nomination or election to any such other elective office.

"SEC. 5. The Representatives from any newly admitted State shall be divided into the two classes described in this article immediately after the House of Representatives shall be assembled in consequence of the first election of Representatives from such State.

"SEC. 6. The provisions of this article shall apply to Representatives elected for terms beginning after one year of the ratification of this article.

"SEC. 7. The first sentence of section 2 of article I of the Constitution of the United States is hereby repealed."

＊　　　＊　　　＊　　　＊　　　＊

drawn to determine the length of term for each member. Members would have to resign their House seats before seeking or accepting the nomination for any other elective office (not just the Senate), unless there was a vacancy in the office sought. In short, there would be no "free crack" at any incumbent of any elective office. (Another version of the staggered-term proposal would have all terms end at the first regular election following reapportionment. Then lots would be drawn again for length of term.)

Those who support the staggered term accept the premise that conditions demand lengthening the term. Society is changing, public problems are complex and demand more time for solution, campaigns are exhausting and expensive. They likewise accept many of the advantages which are listed by the concurrent-term proponents—particularly the electoral advantages to the congressmen. At the same time, the staggered-term proponents express concern about the increased power and stature of the executive relative to Congress and the dangers of the national government becoming increasingly unresponsive to the needs of the people. The happy compromise for them is to have half of the members elected every two years. This system, they believe, will continue to provide expression for the voters every two years and yet members would gain all of the advantages of the four-year term. Further, the House would retain an important measure of independence from the executive since only half of the members would run with the President. And finally, the occasional tidal wave of electoral support for one party would not completely swamp the other party, since half of the House and two-thirds of the Senate would not be up for election.

In effect, the staggered-term proponents accept all of the supporting arguments set forth by the concurrent-term proponents and add one which is specific to their proposal. The Senate has always had staggered elections which contribute to the continuity and prestige of the body; if it works there, it should work for the House.[23]

23. American Enterprise Institute, "Proposals for 4-Year Terms for Members of the House of Representatives," Feb. 18, 1966, p. 15.

THE OFF-YEAR TERM

Even more concerned about the independence of Congress relative to the executive are the proponents of having all members elected at mid-term elections. This proposal would result in the advantages of the long term without the disadvantages of having Congress become more dependent on the executive. Members "would be standing entirely on their own two feet and not being swept in or having their election influenced by the popularity or unpopularity of the presidential candidate of their party."[24] One Brookings round table participant who supported this proposal viewed it as a method which would encourage creativity in the House.

As a result . . . they are not going to be following the dictates with regard to legislation which come from the executive but they are going to be the creative legislative instruments themselves, which is going to make them better students and more effective as law makers and less rubber stamps and less dependent upon what the executive will happens to be.

THE THREE-YEAR TERM

One proposal with limited support suggests a three- rather than a four-year term. Herbert Tenzer (D-New York) was its chief sponsor in the 89th Congress. Many of the same arguments for a change are relied on by Tenzer but in addition he notes that the three-year term "would maintain the essential features of our system of checks and balances" since congressmen would run with the President only once every four elections.[25]

The most attractive feature of a three-year term (aside from the fact that Madison supported it) would seem to be that it would be a compromise between two and four years. Thus, the proposal might be acceptable to both short-term and long-term proponents just as the two-year proposal was in 1787. It is unlikely that the Tenzer amendment will ever be adopted as a com-

24. Subcommittee No. 5, *Hearings*, p. 125.
25. *Ibid.*, p. 39.

promise, however, because there is more involved in the issue than the number of years served. The concurrent-term proponents are certainly not going to accept a proposal which takes the House of Representatives even further from the President than at present. And the staggered-term proponents view their own proposal as a better compromise—one which more nearly meets all needs than the three-year-term proposal. Since there is very limited support in Congress for the three-year term (see Chapter V), and it has so few merits in and of itself, the proposal will receive no further treatment in this study.

Opposition to the Four-Year Term

The opponents to the four-year term have counter arguments for all of those put forward by the proponents. All of these counter arguments can be traced to a fundamental difference of opinion about the job of a congressman and how that job ought to be performed. And the debate over that question today differs little from the debate 180 years ago. The opponents of the four-year term defend the two-year term in very much the same way as Elbridge Gerry defended the one-year term in 1787. The House of Representatives, the short-termers argue, was intended to be close to the people. It is the job of representatives to stay in touch with their constituents so as to reflect their needs, wants, and changes in attitude. It is highly unlikely that members will do this job if they are elected for longer terms. The only way to assure that they will stay close to the people is to force them to come home frequently so as to be reelected. Emanuel Celler (D-New York), Chairman of the House Committee on the Judiciary, opened the 1966 hearings with a strong statement on this subject:

> The House of Representatives is the body nearest to the people—it is the body in which all measures to raise revenue are originated and is closest to the Nation's pocket nerve. . . .
> It is . . . said that no sooner is a Member elected than he must begin campaigning again, for primary as well as regular contests. Why not? It is that campaigning that keeps a Member alive to the issues. He educates the constituent who, in turn, educates him. In other words,

the 2-year term serves as a barometer and that barometer is essential to our system of checks and balances, and this barometer indicates a shift in public opinion which gives a reading to the majority party and emphasizes to the minority the role it must play.[26]

Several round table participants stressed the importance of campaigning and elections for legislating. To them, it was all part of the job:

The representative and legislative function includes as one of its essential parts the reporting back to the people on what you have done and what issues have come up and what your studies in those subjects have revealed. The other part of it is, as a legislator, using your constituents' case histories as grist for the legislative mill. I think 90 percent of the ideas I have had for changing laws have come from the case histories of my constituency. The election process is very much a part of the legislative function.

───

Our discussion of the congressman's role has up to the moment centered too much on the errand-boy half of being a congressman. The other half, I believe, is that of the statesman, the legislator, and here I find that it is very useful to have to run every two years, because this compels a legislator to go home, to do what I do, which is to bend my ear as much as I can, to ring door bells, to find out what people are thinking about Viet Nam, about the war against poverty. They want to expand it or cut it back. They have their reasons about the draft, about inflation, about economic policy, about a million other things, and I doubt very much, considering the clay I am made of, that I would be quite as assiduous in going back and making those rounds if I had to run only once every four years.

Thus, the short-termers respond in one of two ways to the proponents' arguments for a four-year term. Either the proponents' arguments merely support the need for retaining the two-year term or suggest problems which can be taken care of with less drastic reform.

CONDITIONS FOR CHANGE

The short-termers acknowledge that public problems are more complex and that more of them find their way to Washington for

26. *Ibid.*, pp. 145–46.

solution. But far from being conditions requiring longer terms, these are reasons for retaining a system which keeps representatives close to the people. The very complexity of the problems faced in government today demands that frequent reference be made to those who are experiencing these problems.

As for the other two conditions mentioned by the four-year-term proponents—lengthy congressional sessions and the increased costs of campaigning—there are other, less drastic changes which can be made to remedy the situation. Lengthy congressional sessions result from the fact that Congress often meets only three days a week to do its work. Further, it gives itself long holidays throughout the year. Regarding campaign costs, the short-termers point out that a reasonable and enforceable campaign expense law could be enacted to alleviate this real problem. In fact, a four-year term may not be a solution to this problem at all.

ADVANTAGES TO BE GAINED

Recruitment. Short-termers deny that qualified men refuse to run because of the two-year term. "I don't believe that the two-year term has any effect at all upon the availability of talent who want to run for Congress for the first time," is the way one member put it. Several other round table participants, congressmen and staff, agreed with this observation; many noting that they knew of no one who had declined to run for reason of the length of term. But even if it can be demonstrated that men are refusing because of the problems of the two-year term, so much the better for the House of Representatives. In effect, it is argued, these are men who do not want to endure the frustrations of constantly checking with the people through elections, which is the job of the House member.

Elections. Campaign costs are rising and that is a problem which should be attended to, but it can be solved in other ways such as reasonable limits on expenditures, full reporting, tax credits or deductions for contributions, and enforcement of the law.[27] And

27. *Ibid.*, p. 147.

there is certainly no guarantee that a four-year term will cut costs in half. In some cases, due to greater attractiveness of the longer term, increased primary competition may actually increase campaign costs.

The burden of the biennial campaign is part of the job. This, again, is the crux of the matter. To free the representative of these "inexorable pressures" is to change a key feature of our representative government.

Now, I recall that in the President's message he mentioned the fact that 2-year terms tend to keep a Member of the House constantly politically minded and aware of the necessity of going back to his district and keeping in touch with people . . . *that is what we should do.* I mean I think *that is the job,* the purpose of this branch, of the House.[28]

The two other electoral advantages are not considered significant by the short-termers. The reduction of administrative costs for the states is no reason to change the length of term, and national issues are already being discussed in mid-term elections.[29]

Policy Making. The short-termers have very little sympathy for the argument that the President needs more support. If anything, the reverse is true. Congress needs to develop more independence from an executive who has become so powerful.

Checks and balances, I think, are the great obstacles that prevent any department or branch of government from running wild. . . . And when you take away this 2-year term and lodge the legislative responsibilities of the House in Members who have 4-year terms, I think you are removing this very important constitutional concept and contribution to government.

. . . there is a tendency to move government away from the people. I think that the many programs that we have enacted here with increasing number of agencies and expansion of bureaucracies has a tendency to take government away from the people. And this is simply another expansion of that. That is one of the things that makes me most fearful of this proposal . . .[30]

28. *Ibid.,* p. 152; emphasis added.
29. *Ibid.,* p. 203.
30. *Ibid.,* p. 152.

When told that the four-year term will give the representative more time for weighing the problems, and alternative solutions to these problems, the short-termers return once more to their basic argument. It is the job of the representative "to mirror the concerns of his constituency." He cannot do his job in "contemplative seclusion." "Good representation is the creature of good dialogue."[31]

Regarding the supposed advantage of reducing the influence of lobbyists and contributors, opponents of the four-year term point out that one could logically argue just the other way. Frequent elections prevent members from submitting to pressures since they know their behavior is closely watched. Long terms put the member further from the public eye and therefore more susceptible to pressures.

With regard to policy issues, the short-termers point out that the problem of avoiding controversial issues is not solved by the four-year term—only alleviated somewhat. Further, it may well be that these are problems which are not ready for solution in the way proposed. Thus, it is better for the system that congressmen are apprehensive since they are in reality reflecting an apprehensiveness on the part of the public. Finally, those in favor of short terms note that certain problems also get solved because of election-year campaigning which might otherwise have been postponed.

SUPPORTING ARGUMENTS

In the debates of the Constitutional Convention and the dialogue following the writing of the Constitution, the two-year proponents will find more support than the four-year proponents. As for other supporting arguments—that other systems have longer terms and that there is support outside the House—the short-termers are unimpressed. The House of Representatives is not like any other legislature, but even if it were, extending the

31. *Ibid.,* p. 177.

length of House terms would be wrong. And it is questionable the extent to which senators, state legislatures, and the people favor it. Senators fear that House members may run against them during those election years when they don't have to seek reelection in the House. (The President's proposal doesn't remedy the problem because the time limit is thirty days. House members could still run against the incumbent senator in the primary.) What the state legislature would do is anybody's guess. And the people simply haven't formed a judgment based on a full debate of the problem. Even though polls show them in favor, they are soon convinced to change their views. This view was expressed both in the round tables and in the hearings:

> You know, in my speeches at home invariably this question comes back in the "question and answer" period. I sense, and I am pretty sure I am correct, that 80 percent of the audience is in favor of the four-year term because they think it is silly to run every two years . . . I make this simple statement that as I view the Constitution, the House is supposed to represent people directly and as such it is up to us to be close to the people and there is nothing that will get you closer than going out every two years to get yourself elected. . . . Before I am through, I think 80 percent of them agree with me.

> ———

> . . . more information to the people as to how this would directly affect their pocketbooks, how it would definitely affect the public trust of elected officials, how it would affect the majority rule, and how it would affect the principle of separation of powers, in my opinion will bring a complete reversal.[32]

Chairman Celler had a more colorful way of saying the same thing:

> It is very much like a fellow who goes out with a girl. He is very much attracted to her because of her looks, and the second time he goes out with her, he finds that she is ignorant. The third time he goes out, he finds she is bowlegged. The fourth time he goes out, she has a body odor, and finally he discards her.
> MR. HALL. I yield to the chairman's experience.[33]

32. *Ibid.*, p. 279.
33. *Ibid.*, p. 278.

TECHNICAL OBJECTIONS TO THE FOUR-YEAR TERM

Those opposed to the four-year term also raise a number of technical questions—particularly to the staggered elections proposal. Some of the problems raised are not easily resolved.

1. Would Congress organize differently? Many rules would presumably have to be changed. Chairman Celler listed a few of the practical problems, as follows:

Would we have a new Congress every 2 years, or would the House become a continuing body for 4 years? Do bills die at the end of 2 years as they do now, or remain alive for 4? Is the Speaker elected for 2 or 4 years?[34]

2. The staggered elections proposal would result in two classes of congressmen: those always elected in the mid-term and those always elected with the President. ". . . We would have a presidential party and a non-presidential party. Thus the splits already existing in each of the major political parties would be increased."[35]

3. Since House seats are allocated to the states by decennial reapportionment, new and complicated procedures would have to be developed to cope with the problems raised by the four-year term (particularly for the staggered elections proposal). Four-year terms do not coincide with the decennial census, and though the problem could be worked out if all members were elected at the same time, it becomes very complex if the terms are staggered. Under the Chelf proposal, whenever there are changes in a state's apportionment, the members draw lots for length of term. But certain questions need answering. Who draws lots? All the members of the delegation or just those who were elected in the first election following reapportionment? Assume that a state gains one seat in the 1970 census giving that state a total of 11 seats. The state has five members who were elected in 1970 for a four-year term. The legislature redistricts the state prior to the 1972

34. *Ibid.*, p. 147.
35. *Loc. cit.*

elections. What happens to the five who were elected for a four-year term? It is not clear in the Chelf proposal.[36]

There are other ways of handling redistricting. All members might have their terms end with redistricting, regardless of whether they are in the middle of a four-year term or not (one resolution does in fact call for this arrangement). This is undoubtedly the most feasible of the alternatives though it is far from satisfactory. Under this procedure it is quite conceivable that a member elected for four years not only is limited to two but he may well draw another two-year term when the delegation meets to draw lots after the 1972 election.

Another complicated proposal is for those who were elected in 1970, for example, not to run again in 1972, but to participate in the drawing of lots following the 1972 election, so as to keep the delegation evenly divided between those running in presidential and non-presidential years. The problem with this procedure is obvious; a representative could end up with a six-year term by being elected in 1970 and drawing a four-year term in 1972.

Unless one wishes just to ignore the fact that reapportionment will always come when some members of the delegation are in the middle of a four-year term, there are enormous technical complications in any staggered-term proposal.

4. In dividing the state's delegation between those elected in presidential years and those elected in non-presidential years, problems arise in that many states have an uneven number of representatives (17 in 1967). Further, five states (Alaska, Delaware, Nevada, Vermont, and Wyoming) have only one represent-

---

36. Assume, for example, that the districts of the members elected in 1970 were unchanged—that the eleventh member's district was carved out of the five which were up for reelection in 1972. Now the Chelf resolution reads that "all of the Members . . . from that State elected at the first election following the reapportionment shall be divided by lot," so that their length of term may be determined. Presumably this would refer to the five members who were up for reelection in 1972, plus the new member. If three of the six then serve two years and three serve four years, the whole system would be thrown off. There would be *eight* members up for reelection in 1974 (the five elected in 1970, plus three elected in 1972), and only *three* up for reelection in 1976.

ative and thus are denied biennial expression at the polls unless a senator is up for reelection.

MINORITY PARTY OBJECTIONS
TO THE FOUR-YEAR TERM

Members of the minority party make a strong case that a concurrent four-year term system would reduce their chances of victory at the polls and seriously affect the two-party system. Since 1854, the opposition party has been successful in reducing the President's margin in the House in every mid-term election but one, in 1934. The mid-term election provides an important opportunity for the minority party to rebound from presidential election years, when they normally lose seats. Since 1928, the minority Republicans have had a net gain in House seats only twice in presidential election years—1952 (when their presidential candidate won) and 1960.

A statistical demonstration can be contrived that, if it were not for the mid-term elections from 1928 to 1964, the Republican Party would now have only fifty-three members in the House of Representatives! That is, in 1928 there were 267 Republicans in the House. Since then, the Republicans have had a net loss of 214 House seats in presidential election years (losing a total of 256 in 1932, 1936, 1940, 1944, 1948, 1956, and 1964; and gaining a total of 42 in 1952 and 1960). That the Republicans had over three and one-half times that many members in the 90th Congress can be attributed largely to the mid-term election. At least one may expect Republicans to convince themselves of this fact.

Small wonder, then, that the overwhelming majority of minority party members oppose the concurrent-term proposal (see Table 20, Chapter V).

Summary

The proponents of the various forms of a four-year term make a strong logical case in their discussion of the conditions for change and the advantages of change, and in their supporting arguments.

Particularly impressive are the electoral advantages (fewer campaigns, less cost) which all proponents claim will result from the change, and the policy-making advantages (a more coordinated legislative program, less constituency orientation) which the concurrent-term proponents claim for their proposal. The rebuttal in favor of keeping the two-year term is equally strong and is vigorously set forth by a number of key members of the House. Each position has strength because the debate is conducted by serious people who have different views about the job of a congressman, how the job of a congressman ought to be accomplished, the general function of Congress, and how that function ought to be achieved. Both sides rely on arguments which develop logically from certain basic premises, although certain arguments are no more than debaters' points. Their predictions about the advantages or disadvantages of the *four*-year term must, of course, be highly speculative since no one is quite sure what would happen.

It is possible, however, to provide something more than speculation about the effects of the *two*-year term. If one can say something definite about these effects, what they really are, then it should be possible to assess the four-year-term proposal, and other proposals, with more confidence. The rest of this study offers such an assessment, based largely on an examination of the effects of the two-year term on congressional behavior.

CHAPTER
THREE

~~~~~~~

ELECTORAL EFFECTS
OF THE TWO-YEAR TERM

What are the electoral effects of the two-year term on congressional behavior? That is, what effect does the two-year term have
on recruiting able candidates, on the qualifications of members
of the House, on dollar and other costs of campaigning, and on
the number of terms a representative is likely to serve? This
chapter will give some factual evidence on such matters, which
will be useful in assessing the merits of pro and con arguments
about the four-year-term proposal.

Recruiting Candidates

When President Johnson suggested that a four-year term would
"attract the best men in private and public life into competition
for this high office," he was certainly touching on a significant
and sensitive problem in American politics. James D. Barber
nicely summarizes the significance of recruitment:

Perhaps the survival of American democracy does not depend on
recruiting the very best talents to government. But *excellence* in

45

American government—the rationality of its decisions, the quality of justice it dispenses, the timeliness of its actions—these things depend profoundly on the character of those we elect.[1]

But any reform which is justified as likely to recruit qualified men to office seems to suggest that those of the highest quality are not now in office. Thus, the President had to choose his words carefully. He did not say that the four-year term would attract "better men," but "the best men."

Do qualified men decline to serve in the House because of the two-year term? Obviously, this is a hard question to answer. In the first place, it is difficult to agree on standards of quality. Congressmen themselves raised this point in the Brookings round table discussions:

Who determines what a qualified man is? You will find in the House of Representatives, I think, some extremely well-qualified men who have had the least education, and have the least by way of money . . . and yet if you would run it through a computer you would say these men can't run for Congress, they are not qualified, they didn't graduate from Harvard, they didn't do this and that.

It can be argued that the qualities essential to the jobs of governor, judge, or business leader are not those needed in the House of Representatives.

Second, it is exceedingly difficult to collect data on those who decline to run. The implication of the President's four-year term proposal is that qualified men have the opportunity to run and decline for reasons related to the two-year term. Reasons suggested include the need to raise money to run every two years, dislike of campaigning every two years, the likelihood of defeat before reaching a position of influence in a body where seniority is so important, and the adverse effects on family life of campaigns and insecure tenure. There are certainly individuals who have declined to run for such reasons, but when asked specifically for such cases, round table participants had difficulty citing cases. One noted that a former governor refused to run because he "felt it was below his dignity to run for congressman," but there were few other examples.

1. James D. Barber, *The Lawmakers: Recruitment and Adaptation to Legislative Life* (Yale University Press, 1965), p. 1, emphasis added.

On the other hand, several round table participants thought that some members of the House had declined to run for another term, at least in part because of the two-year-term problem.

It is not the problem of recruitment; . . . the glamour of the unknown recruits them. The problem is greater in the staying, in not leaving the job.

Several New York congressmen have accepted judgeships when, according to one congressman, they "would have preferred to stay here if it were a longer term. . . ." In such cases, however, most round table participants had difficulty identifying the two-year term as the principal cause. In the case of New York judgeships, a more typical coment was:

Most of those who went to the bench really preferred the bench and really were looking forward to that; it was a part of the promotional system with which they were operating. Congress is one step in the progression, and it wasn't the two-year term. The same condition would have prevailed if it were a four-year term.

There is a third element—the likelihood of winning—in determining the effect of the two-year term on recruitment. If a candidate has a good possibility of winning, the length of term is not an important consideration. As one Democrat noted, the Republicans never had a problem recruiting an opponent because his was a marginal district. "It was the possibility of winning that prompted them to run." Another round table participant blamed the press—rather than the two-year term—for making the job undesirable, by treating representatives as "secondary politicians."

In brief, it is very difficult to demonstrate the extent to which men who have the kind of qualities needed in the House of Representatives have declined to run for the office, given the opportunity to do so. And it is even more difficult to demonstrate that such men would run if there were a four-year term. Most of the participants in the Brookings round tables—congressmen and staff—either did not consider the two-year term harmful to recruitment or thought that it played only a small role.

I really don't feel that the length of the term has too much to do with this, with whether you run for it or don't run for it.

———

I have never heard . . . any candidate, actual or potential, for the House of Representatives, of either party, give as a reason for not running or as an ingredient in his decision, the fact that it was a two-year term.

———

I don't believe that the two-year term has any effect at all upon the availability of talented men who want to run for Congress for the first time.

Qualifications of Congressmen

What types of men do come to the House of Representatives? It is possible to present data on the educational and occupational background of members, if not on the men who decline to run for House seats. A man's education and occupation are not necessarily valid indicators of his ability to represent and to make laws, but they are often relied on as measures of "quality," and are certainly worth examination, in the absence of any standard test. Members of the House of Representatives in the 89th Congress were well-educated—almost as well-educated as their long-term colleagues in the Senate (Table 4). It is difficult, of course, to say how much education is really necessary for the job, and impossible to conclude that men with little or no college training cannot make good representatives. Indeed, several of the leaders of the House have had no college education. What can be said is that, on the basis of their educational attainments, the House of Representatives is clearly a qualified elite. Further, there seems to be very little difference between the House and the Senate in regard to educational attainment.

The fact that more than half of the senators and representatives in the 89th Congress had law degrees suggests that legal training is an important prerequisite for Congress. One could, of course, logically argue that more occupational diversification is needed. It is doubtful, however, that the President, or other supporters of the four-year term, had this argument in mind when they suggested the possibility of attracting more qualified men to serve in the House.

TABLE 4

College Education of House and Senate Members,
89th Congress, 1966

Level of Education	House		Senate	
No college	29	*7%*	4	*4%*
Some college	62	*14*	13	*13*
BA degree (or equivalent)	83	*19*	14	*14*
Law degree	229	*53*	59	*59*
Advanced degrees	32	*7*	10	*10*
	435	*100%*	100	*100%*

Sources: *Congressional Directory,* 89 Cong., 2 sess. (1966), and *Biographical Directory of the American Congress,* 1774–1961 (U.S. Government Printing Office, 1961).

A profile of occupational backgrounds of congressmen also indicates the extent to which the American people are represented by an elite group. Politics, the law, and business clearly are the principal occupations for congressmen. Teaching experience among members is surprisingly high (Table 5). Perhaps the most striking omission from the table is a labor or workers category. Only two members in the 89th Congress were labor leaders (Joseph G. Minish, D-New Jersey; and Paul J. Krebs, D-New Jersey), and one member (John A. Race, D-Wisconsin) was a machinist. There are no other listings in either house which indicate a labor background. This overrepresentation of certain occupational backgrounds does not necessarily mean that certain interests are favored over other interests, but it would be possible to develop such a hypothesis on the basis of these data.

A comparison between Great Britain and the United States of the occupational backgrounds of legislators shows a high proportion from legal and business professions in both countries, but the laboring classes are much more adequately represented in Britain. Of the 630 members elected to the House of Commons in 1964, 105 (or 17 percent) were workers.[2] All but two of these were members of the Labour Party. If it is true that a more diversified house is a more "qualified" house (a very problematical as-

2. David E. Butler and Anthony King, *The British General Election of 1964* (Macmillan, 1965), pp. 234–39.

TABLE 5

*Occupational Background of House and Senate Members,
89th Congress, 1966*

Occupation[a]	House		Senate	
Civil service/politics	367	*84%*	98	*98%*
Law	238	*55*	67	*67*
Business/banking	123	*28*	24	*24*
Agriculture	34	*8*	16	*16*
Teaching	33	*8*	13	*13*
Journalism	28	*6*	8	*8*
Other	13	*3*	3	*3*

Source: *Congressional Quarterly Weekly Report*, Jan. 1, 1965, pp. 25–29.
[a] Since some members have more than one occupation, the totals exceed 100 percent.

sumption), then the House of Commons shows up better than the House of Representatives. But can this difference be traced to the length of term? Members of the House of Commons do have the potential of nearly a five-year term, but this is an unlikely reason for more working men serving there. There is a Labour Party in Britain which provides a definite avenue into the House for British workers. Also, campaign expenses are strictly limited, the party plays a greater role in providing campaign expenses than in the United States, and the campaign is considerably shorter. These are more likely reasons for greater representation of the working class in Britain.

The previous political experience of senators is generally more impressive than that of House members. In the 89th Congress, forty-four senators had served previously in the House (some for several terms) and eighteen had served as governors of their states. Only three House members (William M. Tuck, D-Virginia; Robert T. Stafford, R-Vermont; and Vernon W. Thompson, R-Wisconsin) had served as governors, and two House members (Alton Lennon, D-North Carolina; and Claude Pepper, D-Florida) had served previously in the Senate.[3]

Obviously, for many members, the House is a stepping-stone to the Senate and, for many governors, the Senate is the only

3. Lennon was appointed to the Senate seat, not elected.

chamber in which they would consider serving. Would this be likely to change if the term of House members were lengthened? It is conceivable that more men with greater political experience would run for the House if the term were four years rather than two, but the Senate would still be more attractive for other reasons. Because there are fewer of them, individual senators have more prestige than House members. Moreover, seniority would continue to be important in the House, and former governors probably would continue to view election to the House as a step down. In short, the Senate attracts men of greater political experience for reasons other than the long term.

There is also some evidence on those who lose congressional races, which is pertinent to recruitment of "qualified" candidates. Robert J. Huckshorn and Robert Spencer studied the losing candidates in the 1962 election and conclude that while many losing candidates are, politically, "poorly prepared, inexperienced, and naive . . . ," they are also well-educated and in high-prestige occupations (although fewer losers are lawyers than winners). Losers run for a variety of organizational, ideological, altruistic, and personal reasons. Given the hopelessness of many races, the small amount of aid the party often gives the candidate, and the inevitable letdown after losing, it is remarkable that so many men of ability do run, just to "fill the ticket."[4]

In a study of nonincumbent candidates in the 1964 election, Jeffery Fishel's data complement those of Huckshorn and Spencer. Nonincumbent candidates are well-educated, are from high-prestige occupations, and are recruited in a variety of ways. They enter politics principally because they wish to serve the community, influence public policy, build a political future for themselves, serve their party, and because they enjoy it—it is a way of life. The local and state party organizations were not viewed by Democratic candidates as being of much assistance to their effort in 1964. The national party, however, was viewed as offering considerable assistance by a surprisingly high percentage of candidates in both parties. Outside the South, most Democrats considered that President Johnson's candidacy helped them, while

4. Huckshorn and Spencer were kind enough to allow me to examine two chapters of their forthcoming book, *The Politics of Defeat*.

most Republicans thought that Barry Goldwater harmed their efforts.[5] In neither study was the two-year term discovered to be an important factor in recruitment.

The sketchy evidence available provides little support for the proposition that better-qualified men would serve in the House of Representatives if the term were four years instead of two. Men of quality are serving in the House of Representatives now. Men of quality, if not political experience, run hopeless races for House seats. What increment, if any, would result from a four-year term is impossible to know. Then, there is no objective standard of measurement for determining quality in representatives. Perhaps even being a governor or a judge is no qualification for being a better member of the House. And while it is true that men of different qualifications serve in the Senate, it cannot be demonstrated that they have chosen that body solely because of the longer term (though it was undoubtedly an important consideration). Thus, the effect of the two-year term on "quality" does not in itself appear to be significant enough to warrant lengthening the term of House members.

Dollar Costs of Campaigning

Lengthening the term for congressmen, it is argued, will reduce the costs of elections and free the member from continuously campaigning for reelection. Of all of the arguments for the four-year term, those related to campaigning seem, on the surface, to have the most validity. That is, it does seem logical that campaigns every four years would cost less and give the member more free time to "do his job." What evidence is there for these alleged benefits?

It is common knowledge that it costs money to get elected to Congress and that the cost continues to increase. Though a few members of Congress doubt the ultimate value of money in gain-

5. Jeffrey Fishel, "Legislative Candidacy and the Political Career" (unpublished Ph.D. dissertation, UCLA, 1966–67).

ing reelection, most would probably agree with this statement by a junior congressman:

> I know what the answer is to the chief problem all of us have—money. When the congressional committee calls me after election and asks what help I need I always say, "Money—that is all I want from you people."[6]

Despite such agreement about the significance of campaign costs, and agreement on certain generalizations about money in elections, there is an incredible lack of data, mountains of misinformation, and a large measure of just plain nonsense about congressional campaign costs. As a result, those who favor longer terms to reduce campaign costs rely more on unvalidated assumptions than on hard facts.

There are few topics in American politics about which less is actually known than congressional campaign finance. Further, what is "known" often cannot be published. Campaign cost data exist, of course, but they are almost impossible to collect for the record.

THE CORRUPT PRACTICES ACT

Certainly, one would not get the facts from the campaign expense reports filed with the House Clerk. The Corrupt Practices Act of 1925 requires each candidate for the House to file pre- and post-election reports on personal campaign receipts and expenditures. Fines and/or imprisonment are the penalties for not filing such reports. Every candidate may spend up to $2,500, but this limit may be as much as $5,000 for the more populous districts, depending on the number of votes cast in the congressional district in the preceding election (calculated on the basis of three cents a vote). How is it, then, that some candidates report more than $30,000 in campaign expenses (see Table 6)? There are two categories of expenses which must be reported: the "itemized" expenses which may not exceed $5,000, *and* the so-called "nonitemized" expenditures. The latter are *not* limited and may be

6. Charles L. Clapp, *The Congressman: His Work as He Sees It* (Brookings Institution, 1963), p. 351.

reported in a single sum which may include such major campaign expenses as travel, stationery, postage, printing costs (except for newspapers or billboards), distribution of letters and circulars, and telephone costs.

Further, the law requires that only campaign expenses made with the "knowledge and consent" of the candidate be reported. Money spent by local, instate committees need not be reported since it is presumably spent on behalf of the candidate without his knowledge or consent.

The result is that the Corrupt Practices Act is not enforced. As shown in Table 6, thirty-eight candidates filed no report at all in 1964. Several others failed to file either the pre- or post-election report. In 1962, fifty-four candidates failed to file any reports. But there is no record of *any* prosecution for failure to meet even these minimal requirements of the law.[7]

It is likely that the Attorney General does not enforce the law because no one is quite sure how to enforce it. Those who fail to report are usually those who have lost (37 of the 38 non-reporters in 1964). Pressing charges against losing congressional candidates is hardly an attractive activity for a busy Department of Justice.[8] And policing *actual* expenditures is virtually impossible; the law is too full of loopholes which permit legal distortion of the amount spent. As Representative James C. Wright, Jr. (D-Texas) testified before the House Committee on Administration, "I daresay there is not a member of Congress, myself included, who has not knowingly evaded its purpose in one way or another."[9]

What Table 6 presents is a breakdown of personal (that is, with the "knowledge and consent" of the candidate) campaign expenses as reported by House candidates in 1964. This table is in

---

7. *Congressional Quarterly Weekly Report*, Jan. 21, 1966, Special Report on 1964 Campaign Contributions and Expenditures, p. 3.

8. *Congressional Quarterly* inquired in a letter to the Department of Justice as to why candidates were not prosecuted. The response was that the policy of the Department is "not to institute investigations into possible violations of [the Act] in the absence of a request from the Clerk of the House of Representatives or Secretary of the Senate." No such requests have ever been made. *Loc. cit.*

9. James C. Wright, Jr., "Let's Revitalize American Democracy," Statement in behalf of the Election Reform Act of 1966 to House Committee on Administration, July 14, 1966 (mimeographed).

TABLE 6

Reported Personal Campaign Expenses
of House Candidates, 1964

Reported expenses	Winners		Losers
	Those with opponents	Those without opponents	
None	39	26	19
$ 0– 5,000	208	14	208
5,001–10,000	77	1	66
10,001–15,000	32	—	25
15,001–20,000	18	—	19
20,001–25,000	9	—	6
25,001–30,000	3	—	4
30,001 or more	7	—	11
No report filed	1	—	37

Source: *Congressional Quarterly Weekly Report,* Jan. 21, 1966, "Special Report on 1964 Campaign Contributions and Expenditures."

no way an accurate indication of campaign expenses. Its interest lies more in what it reveals about the Corrupt Practices Act, because the data are fiction, not fact. It is notable that 39 candidates who won against opposition, and 19 candidates who lost, reported that *no* money was spent in their behalf with their "knowledge and consent."[10]

OFF-THE-RECORD TESTIMONY

Brookings round table participants discussed campaign expenses, and many revealed their best estimates of expenses during the 1964 election. By way of demonstration of the inadequacy of the present law, it is instructive to compare their estimated expenditures with their reported expenditures (see Table 7). There is considerable variation between expenses which the member

10. In Maine, for example, Stanley R. Tupper (R) defeated Kenneth Curtis (D) by a close vote, and against considerable anti-Goldwater sentiment, without any money being spent that he knew about. Curtis also knew of no campaign costs. It must have been a remarkable campaign, even for the taciturn "Maineacs"!

TABLE 7

Estimated "Actual" Expenditures and Reported
Expenditures of Incumbent Candidates, 1964[a]

Identifying number of candidate	Estimated "actual"	Reported
1	$100,000	$15,000–20,000
2	45,000	0– 5,000
3	37,000	5,000–10,000
4	35,000	None
5	34,000	0– 5,000
6	30,000	0– 5,000
7	30,000	25,000–30,000
8	30,000	5,000–10,000
9	20,000	5,000–10,000
10	20,000	None
11	20,000	0– 5,000
12	17,000	5,000–10,000
13	12,500	0– 5,000
14	9,000	0– 5,000
15	8,000	5,000–10,000
16	7,500	0– 5,000
17	5,000	5,000–10,000

Sources: Brookings Round Table Discussions, and *Congressional Quarterly Weekly Report*, Jan. 21, 1966, "Special Report on 1964 Campaign Contributions and Expenditures."
[a] Reported expenditures are in ranges to preserve the anonymity of the individuals. Estimated "actual" figures include the primary election for some members; others had no primary opponent. Primary figures are not required to be reported under Federal law and thus are not in the "reported" column.

had "knowledge" about and what was actually reported. The gap between the two gets narrower as expenses go down; those who spend very little can report everything. It should be emphasized that these discrepancies are not noted here in condemnation of the members, but rather to illustrate the problems in getting accurate campaign cost data—the law actually invites inaccurate reporting.

Some candidates apparently are meticulous about reporting expenses—a few even report committee expenses on their behalf (though they are not required to do so). Seven candidates in 1964 reported personal expenses in excess of $40,000 and one, Roscoe Pickett, Republican, reported expenses of $74,317 in his unsuccessful bid for the seat in the fifth district of Georgia. The problem for enforcement or for relying on these reports for analyzing campaign expenses remains, however, since even those who report large sums may have spent considerably more.

WHAT IS A CAMPAIGN EXPENSE?

If every candidate were to report as honestly and accurately as he could, there still would be serious flaws in the reports as indicators of the costs of campaigning. Is it a campaign expense to send out a newsletter informing constituents about a harbor improvement which you were instrumental in getting for them? Is it a campaign expense to spend money getting twenty times the required number of signatures on your nominating petitions for the primary, when you probably won't even have an opponent? Is it a campaign expense (one borne by the taxpayer) to have your administrative assistant spend time in the district before the election, when Congress is still in session? There are a hundred such questions which might be asked, and different candidates might well answer them differently. The problem is particularly difficult for incumbents since there are often fine lines between what is a campaign expense and what is an expense necessary to being an effective congressman. And if one concludes that the two cannot be separated—that an effective campaigner is an effective congressman—then it can be argued that such expenses are necessary and should be encouraged. (Of course, that line of argument is basic for those who oppose the four-year term.)

Equally difficult to obtain are data about how campaign money is raised. Yet, in assessing the importance of money in congressional campaigning, it is necessary to know where the money came from and how easy or difficult it was to raise. It may well be that a $100,000 campaign fund is easily collected in one district and $20,000 is extremely difficult to raise in another.

EXPENSES DIFFER FROM DISTRICT TO DISTRICT

Despite problems in collecting evidence on congressional campaign cost and analyzing it, it is possible to offer a few generalizations. The most obvious of these is that the amount of money which can be raised and the actual campaign costs differ considerably from one district to the next. Some congressional campaign organizations spend more on postage alone than others do on the whole campaign.

What causes these vast differences in costs? Constituency and candidate-related factors are both involved. First, lack of opposition in the general election will certainly affect campaign expenses, although in uncontested races there may well have been a hotly contested primary. In 1964, there were forty districts in which Democrats had no opponents and one district where the Republican had both the Republican and Democratic nominations. (Forty is a low number of uncontested seats; in earlier years, 100 seats often were uncontested.) Having no opposition does not mean that the winner spends no money in the campaign. Fifteen of the forty-one reported spending some money—eight reported less than $1,000, six reported between $1,000 and $5,000, and one reported $8,424 (Edward A. Garmatz, D-Maryland) (see Table 6).

Second, the strength of the opposing candidate, where there is one, is generally an important factor. Many candidates have only token opposition. Reelection for them is more or less a formality and not particularly costly, although the primary may have been expensive.[11]

Candidates with little or no opposition in the general election may well have opponents in the primary. Expenditures for primaries do not have to be reported at all and yet they may be much higher than general election expenses. Round table participants provided some examples.

> I have run shoestring campaigns in primaries that ran from $25,000 to $35,000. In the general election, I spend maybe $6,000 or $7,500.
>
> ———
>
> You heard about one man from ———, who spent $250,000 to lose an election [a primary], and in the next period, he spent $250,000 to win. In a period of two years, it cost him $500,000 to finally win. I

11. In 1964, for example, 45 Democratic candidates won by a margin of 75 percent or more, and 20 of these won by 80 percent or more. Of the 45, 34 reported spending less than $5,000. See *Congressional Quarterly Weekly Report,* Jan. 21, 1966.

went through the primary campaign, where my adversary originally stated he would spend $250,000. With the campaign over, he boasted of the fact that he spent over $250,000.

Third, various characteristics of the constituency will determine how much money is spent—or has to be spent in order to win. The probabilities are that the most money is spent in tightly contested urban or suburban districts where population density and turnover are high. The problem in proving this assertion is obvious; no reliable data are available.

Fourth, the extent to which the party organization assists the candidate is a factor in how much he personally will spend. If the party assumes part of the cost, the candidate is less pressed to raise money for himself. As one member explained:

I come from an urban community, which is part of an overall election system. My position is part of an organizational framework. And the great bulk of the spending is made by the organization itself.

An interesting colloquy developed on this point:

CONGRESSMAN A: Yours is the same thing, where the organization does everything as far as expenditures of money for the various things are concerned.
CONGRESSMAN B: We still make our contributions to the organizations.
CONGRESSMAN A: But you don't have to raise your own money.
CONGRESSMAN B: Yes, I do.
CONGRESSMAN A: And spend your money.
CONGRESSMAN B: Yes, I do. I go on a fund-raising campaign.
CONGRESSMAN C: What [Congressman A] is trying to say is that in the organizational situation, much more is spent than $10,000 times eight or ten congressmen. . . . The total expenditure of that campaign this fall is greater than that, and to compare what [Congressman A] spends and you spend, you have to include what the organization spends in behalf of all of you as a figure that represents this.

Fifth, newspaper support in the district may make a difference. Some members have strong newspaper backing—others have to pay dearly in order to make up for the fact that the newspapers either ignore them or give them bad publicity. In the round table discussions, one member observed that the newspapers were very friendly to him in that they printed material favorable to him.

Two urban members responded that it cost a great deal to communicate with their constituencies through the mails since the newspapers were unfriendly:

> If I could get done what you do, I would much prefer that to sending out 40,000 mailings but [my paper] won't print what I have got to say, the only way I can get my message out on these issues is through this [mailings]. It is about the only method, other than trying to go around to what meetings you can, but how many people can you see?

> ———

> My weeklies wouldn't even think of carrying a newsletter and I can't get into the [urban] papers, television or radio. I can only get in through the mails.

Other members noted that even friendly newspapers can be expensive in the long run because they expect a pay-off at campaign time:

> With respect to the $20,000 that I spend there is a fairly substantial amount that goes into advertising in the daily newspapers and into the radio ads which, of course, is compensation to them at election time for the benefit that they grant all through the entire two-year period when they take my fifteen minute radio talk every week and my newsletter every week and circulate it among the entire 400,000 who are in the district. It is a necessary part of campaigning although the paid ads, of course, are relatively worthless in relationship to the value of the newsletter and the other non-political coverages I get.

> ———

> The thing that galls me is, these newspapers talk about the terrible costs of campaigns and all that baloney and then they charge double for politicians.

> ———

> I have also found another thing. In the last ten years, we have become a commodity, we have become a customer to those people who sell services like television time, newspaper time, radio time, and the like. These are fellows who are good to us all during the term, they are the news people and the people that we deal with and who put our news releases on the air, and on television, and all, and they will come around during election time and they are trying to sell time. They will say, "Couldn't you give us a little more?"

Finally, there are differences in amounts spent within a constituency between the incumbent and the challenger. There was general agreement among round table participants that if the challenger really wanted to win—even in a marginal district—he would have to spend considerably more than the incumbent. The incumbent has a number of advantages which the challenger must pay for:

> But are we giving any thought . . . to the built-in advantages of the incumbent financed by the federal government with his franking privilege and financed by countless staff workers who can fan out through his district and con the people into all sorts of things? Witness this afternoon the fact that . . . without any real debate or recorded vote, we just voted ourselves a 50 percent increase in our telephone and telegraph allowance, and just last week without any real debate or recorded vote, Congress voted themselves another $7,000 of hatchetman hire.

The result is that challengers, in primaries and general elections, who try hard to win generally must spend much larger sums. Estimates among round table participants varied from three to four times as much as the incumbent to over one hundred times as much.

In summary, it seems clear that the dollar costs of campaigning every two years for *some* congressmen are quite high—though costs differ greatly from district to district. It is even more costly to win the seat in the first place for *some* members. The argument is made that a four-year term would relieve the situation, but as will be noted in Chapter V, there are other alternatives for solving the problem of campaign finance—notably the enactment of realistic regulatory legislation with enforcement and penalties for noncompliance, and legislation to aid all candidates in getting campaign contributions.

Time Costs: Candidate, Family, and Friends

There are many other costs involved in campaigning every two years in addition to money. The time expenditure is considerable for those members who are opposed in the primary and the general election. The election year may well find them constantly preoccupied with reelection. The result is that they travel frequently to the district, campaign in two elections, raise money, and divert staff members from their normal duties to election work. Even if the member does not have primary opposition, however, he often considers it necessary that he spend more time in the district in an election year. And many members campaign in the primary whether they have opposition or not. Would this time expenditure involved in trips back home change if there were a four-year term? Round table participants who favored the four-year term were quite frank about this:

MODERATOR: Would you stop going home if it were a four-year term?
CONGRESSMAN A: Yes. I would probably go only once a month.
CONGRESSMAN B: Yes. This year, which is an election year, I have been going home every weekend. On the off-year, I won't go home more than one weekend out of three.

Once again, there are important differences between constituencies on the matter of how much time must be spent campaigning in the district. Table 8 indicates the number of incumbent congressmen who face no opposition in either the primary or the general election, or both. Though there are many complaints about the primary, a large majority of members do not have primary opposition. Most members do have opposition in the general election, as might be expected, and the number is increasing steadily. But there are some incumbent members each congressional election year who have no opposition in either the primary or the general election.

Despite these figures, which suggest that campaigning is not burdensome to certain members, the proponents of the longer term would argue that there is always the potential of having opposition in two elections in one year. This potential is what tends to create the "campaign-oriented mood" around congressional offices, and this mood can only be dispelled by doing away with one set of elections.

In addition to time and money, it is argued, there are costs involving the candidate's family and friends. Again, there are differences among constituencies. Those members whose districts are relatively close to Washington travel to the district frequently. They are expected to do so. Many of these members

TABLE 8

Incumbents Without Primary or General Election Opposition, *1956–64*

Year	Incumbents seeking reelection	Incumbents with no primary opposition		Incumbents with no general election opposition		Incumbents with no primary or general election opposition	
1956	411	275	*66.9%*	73	*17.8%*	43	*10.5%*
1958	394	286	*72.6*	88	*22.3*	68	*17.3*
1960	403	288	*71.5*	76	*18.9*	58	*14.4*
1962	391	286	*73.1*	57	*14.6*	42	*10.7*
1964	397	. . .		37	*9.3*	. . .	

Sources: Compiled from data in the *Congressional Quarterly Almanacs*, and Richard Scammon (ed.), *America Votes* (Macmillan, 1956, 1958; University of Pittsburgh Press, 1959, 1962, 1964).

have their family home in the district. Freshmen members from marginal districts are hesitant to move their families to Washington for what may well be only a two-year stay. Round table participants discussed the problem, as follows:

You just lose contact with your children during the more valuable and formative times of their lives. You get away from your family and the two lovely daughters that you have. This happened to me and happens to others. It makes a lot of people think twice as they realize that this isn't like it was when I came in 1950.

———

When I first came here . . . my family was back home, and I went back weekends. When adjournment came, I was home for a couple of months and we forgot about the problem. During the second year, after about six weeks, my wife said, "We are going down with you." And they came down for the balance of the year. It wasn't any better because I went to the district every weekend, and then I learned that the best thing to do is leave your family home. It is the best of two filthy alternatives.

The demands on the family of political life are certainly considerable and probably greater for certain of the House members than for other men in public life. Indeed, it may well be that, as one member put it, certain qualified men do not run for the House because "they believe the nature of the life is such that it would be a sufficient break with the pattern they have come to that they are not willing to subject themselves or their families to the types of activities or the pace of activities [in Congress]."

Campaigning and Representation

The debate over the values of campaigning gets right to the core of the dispute between the proponents and opponents of the four-year term. For the short-termers, campaigning is part of the job. The length of term was set at two years so that members would pay heed to constituents; not drift too far from them. Congressmen are, after all, both representatives and legislators.

The four-year-term proponents, on the other hand, express grave doubts about this theory of representation. They doubt very much whether enough is learned in the campaign to warrant having one every second year. It simply is not necessary for the member to return to the voters this often. Indeed, he could perform his job better if he did not. According to the long-termers, there is a sort of psychology to frequent campaigning which tends to influence the entire congressional office. It results in an extreme constituency orientation—among the staff and the congressman himself. The continuous campaign forces the member to an "errand boy" role, in which he answers all constituency requests rapidly, and even finds himself *generating* constituency requests so as to demonstrate his efficiency. At the same time, the member avoids controversial legislative issues which he really ought to be facing. As one round table member explained it:

I do not believe that we are doing a proper service to America as a whole, because in the final analysis, I believe we have, under the representative form of government, a certain representative responsibility to the country as a whole. I don't think we are doing the best job we can do when we are confronted with this job of running back and forth and trying to contact people in this modern day and age.

Unfortunately, as with so many topics on congressional elections, the evidence available on this problem of the value of the campaign is relatively slight. That evidence which does exist suggests that there is very little substantive exchange between the representative and the voter during campaigns. According to a study of congressional representation by Warren E. Miller and Donald E. Stokes, voter awareness of candidates is low and their awareness of issues is virtually nil. They found that 49 percent of their sample knew something about the incumbent candidate and 29 percent knew something about the challenger. But only 24 percent knew something about both candidates. Regarding voter knowledge of issues, Miller and Stokes note that "of detailed information about policy stands, not more than a chemical trace was found."[12]

The Miller and Stokes findings do not prove that there were not policy exchanges during the campaign or that constituents did not bring problems to the congressional candidate which triggered in him some insight into needed legislation. In the campaigns which I have followed firsthand, however, and the sample is too small to allow generalization, only very limited exchange between the candidate and the voters was seen. After comparing campaigns in two vastly different types of constituencies, I concluded that both incumbents

. . . sensed, if they did not know for certain, that victory would come if they worked hard until Election Day. Their efforts were tireless. Despite the difference in techniques, organization, and financial resources, both candidates were trying to establish (or, rather, reestablish) themselves in the minds of party workers and voters as energetic, knowledgeable, educated, capable, aware representatives of the people. They stressed their experience. They talked about their record. They enjoyed being asked to unravel complicated issues. If anything, they—not the constituents—were the instructors. Little or nothing occurred in either campaign to convince the candidates to alter their policy-making behavior in Congress.[13]

The short-termers would likely not be impressed with this evidence—pointing out that in the first place the evidence is just not right. There is exchange, candidates do learn; if not on policy

12. Warren E. Miller and Donald E. Stokes, "Constituency Influence in Congress," *American Political Science Review*, Vol. 57 (March, 1963), p. 54.
13. Charles O. Jones, "The Role of the Campaign in Congressional Politics," in M. Kent Jennings and L. Harmon Zeigler (eds.), *The Electoral Process* (Prentice-Hall, 1966), p. 29.

issues, certainly on the needs and wants of constituents. Further, they would undoubtedly argue that the campaign is not always the best time to see this process in action. Effective members are constantly checking with the constituency, not just in election years. Thus, the short-termers would accept the long-termers' point that there is a psychology of campaigning which ties a man to his district. But they claim this is as it should be and as it was intended to be.

Also, the short-termers would respond that even if the evidence is right, that is still no basis for switching to a long term. Just because the practice does not square with the ideal is no reason for abandoning the ideal. Indeed, it is an argument for intensifying the effort of communicating with the people back home. Ignorance on the part of the constituents may be indicative of the fact that the congressman is not doing his job. A dialogue on this very matter occurred during one of the round tables:

CONGRESSMAN A: Any one of us can consider the campaigns that we have been in—and the difficulty of really developing a situation where you can . . . actually cut down a dialogue on government to the point where opposing candidates are being tested on the real differences in their approach to government. It is a rare campaign. . . . I think that [Congressman B] talks of a very ideal situation as he . . . has been able to develop it to some extent but also possibly as he would wish it were rather than how it really is.

MODERATOR: A very good point.

CONGRESSMAN B: Yes, it is, but let's don't cast ideals aside. You never attain an ideal but there is a guiding star that directs the course. . . . Sure I am talking in ideal terms. I don't attain it but I try to seek it. I wish others would, too. I certainly think a political scientist should . . . be concerned about what these guiding stars are. I am so discouraged by the political scientists as a group in their elimination, almost, of these guiding stars of what a legislative body might be, and reducing it to the worst sort of a level, of the wheeling and dealing kind of thing.

The long-termers, on the other hand, probably find support for their argument in the evidence cited above. If the voters are not paying any attention anyway, why force the member to go through the torture of continuous campaigning? He will spend his time much more profitably by working on legislative issues in Washington rather than constantly feeling that he must return home to handle every little detail for constituents.

Campaigning and Tenure in Office

One might well be misled by the arguments in this debate over length of term into believing that there is considerable turnover of House seats each election. In fact, the large majority of incumbent members have a very good chance of being reelected over and over again (though it should be noted that the actual figures will vary between parties since most of the losses are suffered by one party—e.g., the Republicans in 1964, the Democrats in 1966). The membership of the House of Representatives is quite stable. Though it is not a continuing body in the same sense as the Senate, it is continuing in that a new House is made up of most of the members of the old House. The incumbent advantage mentioned earlier seems to pay off at the polls.

Table 9 shows the number of incumbents who were successfully returned in the last six congressional elections. Of those members who seek reelection (generally about 90 percent of the total membership), only a very few are defeated in primaries. The greatest number of members defeated in primaries during the period measured was in 1962 when six were defeated outright and five were defeated when redistricting put them in with other incumbents. Three members lost primaries in 1964 to other incumbents as well. But, of course, redistricting is just another of the problems for House members.

The figures vary somewhat more on incumbent losses during the general elections. The 1956 and 1962 elections left the House very much as it had been before the election. The 1960 election increased the Republican margin somewhat, and the 1958 and 1964 elections were strong Democratic years—many Republican incumbents were ousted. In all, the percentage of members reelected is high, ranging from nearly eighty-seven percent in the Democratic sweep of 1964 to nearly ninety-five percent in

TABLE 9

Number and Percentage of Incumbents
Who Won Reelection, 1956–66

Year	Total incumbents seeking reelection	Those who lost the primary		Those who lost the general election		Those who were reelected	
1956	411	6	*1.5%*	16	*3.9%*	389	*94.6%*
1958	394	3	*0.8*	37	*9.4*	354	*89.8*
1960	403	5	*1.2*	26	*6.5*	372	*92.3*
1962	393	11	*2.8*	14	*3.6*	368	*93.6*
1964	397	8	*2.0*	44	*11.1*	345	*86.9*
1966	407	5	*1.2*	40	*9.8*	362	*89.0*

Source: Compiled from data in the *Congressional Quarterly Almanacs*.

1956. In fact, about as many members retire voluntarily, or do not seek reelection for other reasons, as are actually defeated at the polls.

Just because a surprisingly high percentage of incumbents are returned each election does not mean that all of those running consider themselves reassured of victory. The psychology of the two-year term remains. No one can be sure that he won't be among those few who are defeated.

There is, however, further evidence to ease the minds of those who are preoccupied with reelection woes. The trends seem to favor more and more stability, less and less turnover. An examination of party turnover in congressional districts shows that between 1932 and 1940, 69.9 percent of the districts were won by the same party in all five elections; between 1942 and 1950, 74.0 percent were won by the same party; and between 1952 and 1960, 78.2 percent were won by the same party. The trend is clear and steady—toward less party turnover in congressional districts.[14]

Professor Nelson W. Polsby provides evidence supporting the

14. Charles O. Jones, "Inter-Party Competition for Congressional Seats," *Western Political Quarterly*, Vol. 17 (Sept., 1964), pp. 461–76. See also H. Douglas Price, "The Electoral Arena," in David B. Truman (ed.), *The Congress and America's Future* (Prentice-Hall, 1965), pp. 32–51; and Milton C. Cummings, Jr., *Congressmen and the Electorate* (Free Press, 1967).

conclusion that membership in the House is more of a career for more men now than in the past. Before 1900 the average term of service for all House members never exceeded 2.79 terms. It has never fallen below 3.10 in this century, and since 1955 it has always exceeded five terms. Before 1900, freshmen often constituted half of the membership of the House (and never less than 30 percent), whereas since 1900, the number of freshmen has exceeded 30 percent in only four of the thirty-three congresses, and typically has averaged less than 20 percent in recent congresses.[15]

TENURE OF FRESHMAN CONGRESSMEN

One argument which is relied on by the long-term proponents is that the two-year term does not give freshmen members of the House enough time to learn the job. A four-year term would give them more time to "settle in" before campaigning again. How safe is the freshman congressman? How likely is it that he will be defeated in his attempt to become a sophomore? Table 10 indicates that although the freshman member does not have much to fear from the primary, he needs to be more concerned about the general election than his more senior colleagues. On the basis of the last six elections, it appears that between 70 and 90 percent of the freshmen who are seeking reelection will be returned to office. (Again, there are differences between parties—e.g., Republicans account for most of the losses in 1964, Democrats in 1966.) Many freshmen were turned out in 1960 and 1966. A number of Democrats had won normally Republican seats in the Midwest in 1958 and 1964 and were ousted in 1960 and 1966. The high percentage of those reelected in 1962 coincides with a similarly high percentage in Table 9 for 1962. The freshman score would have been even higher had it not been for redistricting. Two freshmen were defeated in all-incumbent primary races in which two incumbents were thrown into the same district.

15. Nelson W. Polsby, "The Institutionalization of the U.S. House of Representatives," paper delivered at the 1966 Annual Meeting of the American Political Science Association; Statler-Hilton Hotel, New York City, September 6–10, Tables I and II. See also Samuel P. Huntington, "Congressional Responses to the Twentieth Century," in David B. Truman (ed.), *The Congress and America's Future* (Prentice-Hall, 1965), pp. 8–10.

TABLE 10

Percentage of Freshmen Who Won Reelection, 1956–66

Year	Total freshmen seeking reelection	Those who lost the primary		Those who lost the general election		Those who were reelected	
1956	48	1	2.1%	6	12.5%	41	85.4%
1958	38	0		7	18.4	31	81.6
1960	74	0		15	20.3	59	79.7
1962	52	2	3.8	3	5.8	47	90.4
1964	61	1	1.6	10	16.4	50	82.0
1966	79	0		25	31.6	54	68.4

Source: Compiled from data in the *Congressional Quarterly Almanacs.*

Whether it is the result of frequent campaigning, or for some other reason, a high percentage of incumbents are returned to office over and over again. Campaigning becomes part of the job for them. This does not mean that there are no risks in having to run for office every two years, or that a congressman can simply sit back and rely on the data presented here to get him reelected. It does mean that the House membership is quite stable and that the large majority of incumbent members can count on reelection if they conduct an active campaign and capitalize on their incumbency. As one member put it:

There is no question but that an incumbent has strong advantages. He has a forum by virtue of being a congressman, and of course he also has the frank. These are two very important items. At the same time I would point out that sometimes you cannot fight the trend. A good example is 1958. Some representatives got caught in that trend and were replaced by men far inferior.[16]

Summary

This analysis has clarified the extent to which there are adverse effects from the two-year term. The effect on recruitment is apparently negligible, and thus this argument for a longer term is

16. Clapp, *op. cit.,* p. 333.

set aside. The effect on campaign costs is considerable, but analysis is hampered by the lack of reliable data. Further, the data which do exist clearly indicate that the effect is not uniform for all congressional districts. It is also apparent that there are adverse effects on family life for some members who have to campaign frequently. In and of itself, however, this list of effects is not an adequate justification for a change in the length of term.

It is also apparent that few campaigns are characterized by the kind of issue exchange claimed by short-term proponents; frequent campaigns cannot be justified solely on that basis. On the other hand, a "campaign-oriented mood" can develop from frequent elections which influences the congressional behavior of some members. Finally, frequent campaigns are irksome but they do not have to prove uniformly burdensome to all members. The overwhelming majority of incumbents are reelected over and over again.

In summary, though there are adverse electoral effects of the two-year term for certain members, it is highly questionable whether they warrant lengthening the term to four years. Indeed, there is considerable doubt regarding the extent to which a four-year term would relieve many of these effects, and very little evidence to indicate what additional adverse effects would result from the change. Thus, it is not possible to know for certain whether the four-year term would be more helpful than harmful, or vice versa, with respect to the electoral process.

CHAPTER
FOUR

~

POLICY EFFECTS
OF THE TWO-YEAR TERM

All proponents of the four-year term express concern over the effects of the two-year term on policy-making. Those who favor having the members run with the President are concerned about the effect of the off-year election on the presidential program. A president deserves to have a majority on which he can rely, they say, and "divided responsibility should be avoided." Mid-term elections can divide the executive from Congress. Also, the two-year term leaves the member with too little time for studying public problems and legislation. A four-year term would relieve him of the continual burden of campaigning, so that he and his staff could spend more time on legislative tasks. And a longer term would encourage the House to tackle more controversial issues, since the number of elections would be reduced.

The advocates of a staggered four-year term, on the other hand, agree that the latter two effects exist, but they do not wish to give the President any more power over Congress than he already has. Thus, they are not persuaded that all members should run with the President. The two-year termers simply reject all three assertions.

Several sets of data will be examined in this chapter so as to determine what are, in fact, the policy effects of the two-year term. Four problems will be examined: House support for presidential programs, the extent to which controversial legislation is avoided, how the member allocates his time, and what the staff does.

Congressional Support of Presidential Programs

The first evidence to set forth is that on the frequency of party division between Congress and the presidency. How often has the President lost control of Congress during the mid-term elections? During presidential elections? How often has his party's margin been reduced in mid-term elections? During presidential elections? How often has his party's margin been increased? Table 11 presents those data for this century.[1]

There is ample support for the conclusion that the President is more likely to have a majority from his own party in Congress when members run with him. Only once in this century has the President's party increased its margin in both houses during a mid-term election, whereas in nine of the sixteen presidential election years, the President's party has increased its margin in both houses. Conversely, the President's party has had its margin reduced in both houses in thirteen of the seventeen mid-term elections and in only two of the sixteen presidential year elections. The President has never lost control of both houses in a presidential election year in this century, though in 1956 President Eisenhower failed to regain control of Congress after it had been lost to the Democrats in 1954. There is a clear advantage to the President's party in Congress during the presidential election years (although not necessarily attributable to the coattail effect).[2]

1. See American Enterprise Institute, "Proposals for 4-Year Terms for Members of the House of Representatives," Feb. 18, 1966, pp. 18–19.

2. See Warren E. Miller, "Political Coattails: A Study in Political Myth and Methodology," *Public Opinion Quarterly*, Vol. 19 (Winter 1955–56), pp. 352–68; Malcolm Moos, *Politics, Presidents, and Coattails* (Johns Hopkins Press, 1952); and Angus Campbell and Warren E. Miller, "The Motivational Basis of Straight and Split Ticket Voting," *American Political Science Review*, Vol. 51 (June, 1957), pp. 293–312.

TABLE 11

Success of President's Party in Congressional Elections, 1900–66[a]

Election year	Margin of President's party in the Senate	in the House
Presidential election year		
1900	Remained the same	Increased
1904	Remained the same	Increased
1908	Decreased	Decreased
1912	Increased	Increased
1916	Decreased	Decreased
1920	Increased	Increased
1924	Increased	Increased
1928	Increased	Increased
1932	Increased	Increased
1936	Increased	Increased
1940	Decreased	Increased
1944	Remained the same	Increased
1948	Increased	Increased
1952	Increased	Increased
1956	Remained the same	Decreased
1960	Increased	Increased
1964	Remained the same	Increased
Mid-term election year		
1902	Decreased	Decreased
1906	Increased	Decreased
1910	Decreased	Decreased[b]
1914	Increased	Decreased
1918	Decreased[c]	Decreased[c]
1922	Decreased	Decreased
1926	Decreased	Decreased
1930	Decreased	Decreased
1934	Increased	Increased
1938	Decreased	Decreased
1942	Decreased	Decreased
1946	Decreased[c]	Decreased[c]
1950	Decreased	Decreased
1954	Decreased[c]	Decreased[c]
1958	Decreased	Decreased
1962	Increased	Decreased
1966	Decreased	Decreased

Source: *Congress and the Nation, 1945–1964* (Congressional Quarterly Service, 1965).
  [a] Changes are measured by the number of members a party had after each election. Changes which may have occurred between elections are not accounted for.
  [b] President's party lost control of the House of Representatives.
  [c] President's party lost control of Congress.

A greater margin in Congress for the President's party does not translate directly into greater presidential support. The next evidence to examine, therefore, is the extent to which the President receives support for his program from Congresses elected at different times. The *Congressional Quarterly* has been compiling comparative presidential support scores and box scores on legislation since the 83rd Congress, in 1952. These data are pertinent to the present problem. Seven Congresses have been elected since 1952—four during presidential election years and three during mid-term election years.

First, it is necessary to determine how well the President does with Congress. The *Congressional Quarterly* has two methods for determining this—the President's legislative box score (the percentage of his requests enacted into law), and the percentage of roll calls won by the President (that is, where he has taken a stand in favor or against). Table 12 indicates the President's scores by these two measures, 1953–66. There is additional evidence here to support the case of the four-year-term proponents. The mean box score for all presidential requests during Congresses elected with him is 54.5 percent, compared with 39.8 percent during Congresses elected in the mid-term. The mean presidential support score for all roll calls during Congresses elected with the President is 82.4 percent, compared with 73 percent for Congresses elected in the mid-term. Thus, during this time period Congress generally provided the President with more support during the first two years of his administration.

If the Eisenhower administration and the Kennedy-Johnson administrations are examined separately, however, the generalization is modified somewhat. Rather sizable differences continue to exist between presidential box scores for presidential Congresses and mid-term Congresses for both administrations (see Table 13). Based on these very limited data, it appears that the President has considerably more difficulty getting his requests through mid-term Congresses. Having gotten a bill to the roll call stage, however, Presidents Kennedy and Johnson were equally successful in winning majorities in both presidential and mid-term Congresses. As noted in Table 13, Kennedy-Johnson had an average presidential support score of 85.3 during presi-

TABLE 12

Presidential Scores with Congress, 1953–66

Congress	Legislative requests			Roll calls		
	Total number	Number enacted	Percentage enacted	Total number	Number won	Percentage won
Presidential Congresses						
83rd, 1 sess. (1953)	44	32	72.7	83	74	89.2
83rd, 2 sess. (1954)	232	150	64.7	115	90	78.3
85th, 1 sess. (1957)	206	76	36.9	117	80	68.4
85th, 2 sess. (1958)	234	110	47.0	148	112	75.7
87th, 1 sess. (1961)	355	172	48.4	189	154	81.5
87th, 2 sess. (1962)	298	133	44.6	185	158	85.4
89th, 1 sess. (1965)	469	323	68.9	274	255	93.1
89th, 2 sess. (1966)	371	207	55.8	228	180	79.0
Total	2209	1203	54.5	1339	1103	82.4
Mid-term Congresses						
84th, 1 sess. (1955)	207	96	46.3	93	70	75.3
84th, 2 sess. (1956)	225	103	45.7	99	69	69.7
86th, 1 sess. (1959)	228	93	40.8	175	91	52.0
86th, 2 sess. (1960)	183	56	30.6	129	84	65.1
88th, 1 sess. (1963)	401	109	27.2	186	162	87.1
88th, 2 sess. (1964)	217	125	57.6	149	131	87.9
Total	1461	582	39.8	831	607	73.0

Source: Compiled from data in *Congressional Quarterly Almanacs* for relevant years.

TABLE 13

Average Presidential Scores with Congress, Eisenhower and Kennedy-Johnson Administrations

	Eisenhower		Kennedy-Johnson	
	Presidential Congresses	Mid-term Congresses	Presidential Congresses	Mid-term Congresses
$\bar{x}$ Box score	51.4	41.3	55.9	37.9
$\bar{x}$ Presidential Support Score	76.9	63.3	85.3	87.5

Source: Compiled from data in *Congressional Quarterly Almanacs*.

dential Congresses and a remarkably high average support score of 87.5 during mid-term Congresses. President Eisenhower had much less success with support scores during his mid-term Congresses (13.6 less than in presidential Congresses).

What was the source of the difficulty for President Eisenhower? The principal problem was that too many Democrats were elected during the mid-term elections. His own party continued to support him at the same level as during presidential Congresses (see Table 14), but two trends cut into his congressional support—more Democrats were elected, *and* the average support score for Democratic congressmen went down. During the Kennedy-Johnson administrations, Democrats were able to maintain large majorities (at least until 1966) and high presidential support scores.

Thus, it appears that the two-year term can very definitely have an effect on the presidential program. Important differences in congressional support of the President between presidential Congresses and mid-term Congresses can develop. The biennial elections are particularly troublesome for a minority party President (Eisenhower) since if he has a majority in Congress at all, it is likely to be a very small one. There is a high probability, therefore, that the expected loss of seats for the presidential party in Congress during mid-term elections will result in the loss of control of Congress. A majority party President, on the other hand, will probably bring with him a large majority in Congress and therefore he does not face quite the same mid-term election problem as the minority party President. There are further difficulties of analysis, however. The legislative box score for President Kennedy in 1963 (see Table 12) was the lowest of any during the period measured. At the same time it should be noted that Kennedy made many more requests than Eisenhower had ever made, and that many of these requests were enacted into law in later sessions.[3]

3. This point raises some question about the usefulness of these scores. A President may have high scores because he proposes only what he thinks Congress will pass—regardless of whether the problem is solved or not. Another President may score low because he is supporting innovative solutions which later are accepted after he leaves the White House.

TABLE 14

House Presidential Support Scores by Party, 1954–66

Congress and date	President's party		Opposition party	
	Presidential Congresses	Mid-term Congresses	Presidential Congresses	Mid-term Congresses
83rd 1954	71		44	
84th 1955		60		53
1956		72		52
85th 1957	54		49	
1958	58		55	
86th 1959		68		40
1960		59		44
87th 1961	73		37	
1962	72		42	
88th 1963		72		32
1964		74		38
89th 1965	74		41	
1966	63		37	

Source: Compiled from data in *Congressional Quarterly Almanacs*.

The proponents of concurrent four-year terms, with the President, do have evidence in support of their contentions. Even where there is no decline in presidential support following biennial elections, it is obvious that the potential of creating an anti-administration Congress is always present. It may well be that there would be a decline in presidential support during the last two years of an administration anyway, but it seems much less likely if the same majority is to serve throughout the four years than if changes are made.

This evidence can also be used to support the arguments of the short-termers and those who fear the staggered and off-year proposals. They would argue that any decrease in presidential support which comes from a loss of seats by the presidential party or a change in attitude by presidential party members following the mid-term is perfectly in order. Indeed, that is the purpose of the mid-term election. One Republican round table participant even made this point about his own administration:

After the Republican Congress came in it lasted only two years and then the people had a chance to express themselves and voted the Republicans out. This off-year national referendum which is in effect a measure of the public sentiment about the administration, I think, is a very valuable thing.

Once again, it should be emphasized that vastly different interpretations of the job of a representative and executive-legislative relations influence the reactions of these groups to various aspects of the length-of-term issue. There are definite negative policy effects for the President in the two-year term. Whether they are "adverse" or not is debatable.

Controversial Legislation

Another argument for a longer term is that House members would be less hesitant to act on controversial legislation because elections would be less frequent. With elections occurring every two years, it is asserted, such legislation is shelved because members do not want to go on record as favoring or opposing. Presumably this is legislation which results in conflicts for the congressmen, since they believe that constituents are divided on the issue. Voting either way would, in the member's analysis, lose him votes. Thus, he prefers to avoid recording himself one way or the other.

If true, the argument above is a persuasive one in favor of a longer term. Certainly, the four-year term would not completely eliminate any such phenomenon; only reduce its frequency. As one member noted, "Give us a year. The fourth year is still a tough one." But even reducing the avoidance of legislative action because a bill is controversial seems to be an attractive reason for change.

What is the record on this matter? Does the House avoid controversial legislation during election years? As with so many assertions by the long-term proponents, hard evidence is uncommonly difficult to collect. Individual members can cite legislation which, in their opinion, has been shelved because of election year politics. Several did so during round table discussions (see Chapter II). It is true that controversial legislation often is not acted on in election years. But what is in question is the extent to which such legislation is not acted on in election years, contrasted with nonelection years. It should also be possible to identify, as the cause for nonaction, the fact that members do not wish to record themselves because of election-year politics.

Table 15 presents the percentages of presidential legislative proposals (presumably the major source of controversial legislation) which were either accepted or rejected by Congress, 1953–66, divided into election and nonelection years. Given the assertion above, it would be logical to expect that Congress would put itself on record less during election years. In fact, the percentages are greater for election years in four of the seven Congresses where the figures are available for both sessions—the reverse of what one might expect. Overall, 68.4 percent of all presidential proposals during the election years measured were either accepted or rejected; 61.4 percent were either accepted or rejected during nonelection years. Thus, this type of gross analysis of presidential proposals fails to provide any proof of the assertion that controversial legislation is avoided during election years. In fact, the figures seem to indicate that many measures are held over from the first to the second session before final action is taken—perhaps because they are complex and controversial.

It may be that those presidential proposals which do not receive final action in election years are controversial, while those which do not receive final action in nonelection years are not controversial. Any proof of this conclusion would depend on one's judgment as to what is controversial legislation. If such legislation is defined as being of national importance, having widespread effect, and characterized by opposing interests, then it does not seem that the conclusion can be supported by the evidence. A review of specific legislation which did not receive final action by Congress during the years 1962 to 1965 simply does not support the proposition that controversial legislation is avoided in election years.[4] Many of the major controversial proposals

4. The *Congressional Quarterly* has, since 1962, included sections on "What Congress Did Not Do" in the year-end *Almanac*. The conclusions in this paragraph are based on an examination of those policy issues.

TABLE 15

Presidential Requests Accepted or Rejected, 1953–66[a]

Congress	Nonelection year	Election year
83rd	1953—*79.5*%	1954—*85.8*%
84th	1955—*54.1*	1956—*62.7*
85th	1957—*48.1*	1958—*71.8*
86th	1959—*61.8*	1960—*53.0*
87th	1961—*66.8*	1962—*60.1*
88th	1963—*42.6*	1964—*64.1*
89th	1965—*80.6*	1966—*75.7*

Source: *Congressional Quarterly Almanacs.*
[a] Includes all bills rejected in committee or on the floor of either house.

which were neither passed nor defeated in those years were "hardy perennials." Such measures as federal aid to education, medical care for the aged, civil defense, area redevelopment, minimum wage, labor legislation of various types, were shelved *both* in election years and nonelection years. They were not acted on because many of the issues could not be resolved satisfactorily to all of the interests involved.

Perhaps the President does not propose controversial legislation during election years and does in nonelection years. That assertion, while perfectly logical, makes a different point from that set forth by the long-term proponents. Congress is not avoiding legislation if legislation is not proposed in the first place. It is probably true that the President will try to capitalize on his electoral victory in the first year of his presidency and introduce a wide variety of measures—particularly if his majority is as large as Lyndon B. Johnson's in 1964. But he will likely do that anyway; regardless of whether House members are elected for a two- or four-year term.

In conclusion, it is no doubt true that the House does not act on certain controversial measures during an election year because certain members are concerned about making a record which could conceivably hurt them. Indeed, round table participants gave examples of legislation which, in their opinion, was held up for these reasons. The problem becomes one of proving that the practice exists to such an extent that it is necessary to change the length of term for House members. A hunch is not enough to prove the case. And even where one can demonstrate that the practice exists, with specific examples, one can also point to cases which upset the generalization. Thus, in 1966, the "situs picketing" bill was given as an example, by round table participants, of a bill which was too "hot" to be voted on. But, on the other hand, the House spent over a week in 1966 debating, revising, and voting on a major civil rights bill—the third major civil rights bill in three years.

The Time Problem

There is another policy-related argument in support of a longer term—that the member would have more time to devote to considering various alternative solutions to public problems. Freed from at least one set of campaigns, the argument goes, the member could turn his attention to legislative duties, and the result would be beneficial for the nation. But how do members allocate their time now? And what are they likely to do with whatever extra time they would have from a longer term?

The first point to make is, of course, that the allocation of time by a representative will depend upon a number of factors. The committee assignment of the member may be important. Membership on certain committees, notably Ways and Means and Appropriations, may be time consuming. Other committees have more limited responsibilities. The member's seniority and leadership post, if any, may determine in part how he allocates his time. Other factors of importance may include the various political, economic, and geographical characteristics of the constituency. As noted in Chapter III, not every member has a tightly contested primary and general election to engage his attention. Thus, some members have more time to devote to legislation than others because of the political situation in the district. Districts also differ considerably in terms of economic problems which require the attention of the member. Geographical considerations also play a role. Those districts in the East which are near Washington (particularly those in nearby Maryland and Virginia; many of whose constituents phone in their problems) require constant servicing by their members. On the other hand, Far West districts require lengthy travel time on the part of the member. And obviously, during the election year, the member with an opponent must focus his attention on the district. If he faces a stiff challenge, the member, and his staff, may be completely preoccupied with reelection activities.

There are many other possible determinants of how a man allocates his time—e.g., temper of the times, whether his party controls the White House and Congress, pressure group activity —but perhaps the most important of all is how the member views the job. Several colloquies developed during the round table discussions between members who took opposing views on how a representative should spend his time (see Chapter II). The principal disagreement was on how much time ought to be spent on constituency service:

CONGRESSMAN A: [Congressman B], as much as I love you, I find myself in very substantial disagreement with you. I just do not agree that that particular activity is the primary function of a legislator.

CONGRESSMAN B: Which activity? I said there were two primary activities.

CONGRESSMAN A: You referred to one about the contact with the constituents, the so-called running of errands . . . I don't think that is one of our primary functions.

CONGRESSMAN B: Then we do disagree.

CONGRESSMAN C: I don't know how I can be a better legislator if someone wants me to get him out of the armed services or a promotion or get him a transfer or other problems that they come to me with that have nothing to do with legislation. I don't see how it makes me a better legislator. It doesn't give me any idea of what they are thinking about, whether a piece of legislation is good or bad or indifferent.

CONGRESSMAN B: [Congressman C], you are assuming by this last argument that the congressman's job is solely that of a legislator, and I insist that a congressman's job is not that of a legislator only. It is a two-pronged job. He is a representative of his people, not only in terms of representing them in legislation, but in terms of representing them in the executive branch.

CONGRESSMAN C: You are destroying the concept of division of authority between the legislature, judiciary, and executive.

This colloquy well illustrates the difference between those members who think that it is important to concentrate on legislation and those who think that it is important to combine that effort with constituency service. Both types of members are basically oriented toward legislative functions—they only differ on methods. But there are other types of members too—those who are playing to a different audience and are less oriented toward legislative functions. First, there are those who view their service in Congress as being temporary. They are anxious to move elsewhere. Membership in Congress is a means to an end. One round table participant was particularly upset about those who are seeking national office. "They are misusing their positions, just like Bobby Kennedy going abroad when the Senate is in session. These are not the work horses in the legislative process."

Second, there are those who continuously campaign for reelection whether they need to or not. There are cases of members who "over-communicate" with and "over-solicit" the constituency to such an extent that they never have time to legislate. Indeed, as one staff member noted, some members generate constituency service matters and other trivia so that they will have an excuse for not legislating. How many legislators work hard to represent their districts in the legislative process, in the classical model of the district-oriented representative? One member who strongly subscribes to the model gave his assessment:

> Increasingly fewer, but I would say surprisingly (maybe I can't use that adjective because I don't know what people anticipate; I base it on how many of my 435 colleagues are students) many. I give them a pretty good billing. *I would say about half.* I would say there are over a hundred damned good students in the Congress.

The member's interpretation of his responsibilities, therefore, becomes very important in determining how he will use his time. There is no "boss" to define his job for him.

How do most members use their time? This is an exceedingly difficult question to answer, since, apparently, no careful time-study has been done on Congress. One thing is certain: House members do not spend a great deal of their time on the House floor; they are in committee meetings, or otherwise engaged.

One of the conditions which presumably makes the four-year term essential, is that congressional sessions are longer now. There have been long sessions in recent years, as there were during the immediate post-World War II years, but the average number of hours in session has varied little since 1947 (see Table 16). Since 1960, the House has been in session for an average of 160 days a year and 620 hours a year, for an average day of 3.9 hours. The Senate normally is in session more often than the House and the average day is longer. Assuming that there are 250 working days in a year (excluding weekends and holidays) and further assuming that the member gets 30 additional days' vacation, that still leaves the member 60 days (again excluding weekends and holidays) for campaigning if the House is in session for 160 days. And if the member works an eight-hour day, he has considerable time for legislative, committee, and constituency work, since the House is in session only half of that time and he will normally go to the House floor only when his presence there is required. Proponents of the four-year term would point out, however, that the number of days that the House is in session does not provide an accurate indication of the problem. The House does not stay in session the first 160 working days of the year and adjourn in August. When it is in session for 160 days, it generally does not adjourn until October or perhaps even later. Thus, campaigning has to be worked into the schedule of other duties. Blocks of time for campaigning, or for contemplating, are simply not available when the House is in session for long periods of time.

Davidson, Kovenock, and O'Leary asked the members they interviewed to name their most time-consuming activity and important secondary activities. The results are included in Table 17. Note that only 3 percent listed "campaigning" as a major activity, and 14 percent listed it as a secondary activity. But if "campaigning" is defined more broadly, to include case work, errands, communication with the district, then the percentages are increased considerably. These broadly defined campaign activi-

TABLE 16

Time in Session, 1947–64

Year	House			Senate		
	Days in session	Hours in session	Hours in average day	Days in session	Hours in session	Hours in average day
1947	144	686	4.8	143	808	5.7
1948	110	538	4.9	114	654	5.7
1949	165	704	4.3	186	1,145	6.2
1950	180	797	4.4	203	1,265	6.2
1951	163	705	4.3	172	997	5.8
1952	111	458	4.1	115	651	5.7
1953	117	507	4.3	125	764	6.1
1954	123	526	4.3	169	1,198	7.1
1955	112	471	4.2	105	560	5.3
1956	118	466	4.0	119	802	6.7
1957	141	585	4.2	133	861	6.5
1958	135	562	4.2	138	1,015	7.4
1959	141	527	3.7	140	1,010	7.2
1960	124	512	4.1	140	1,188	8.5
1961	147	570	3.9	146	1,005	6.9
1962	157	657	4.2	177	1,159	6.6
1963	186	626	3.7	189	1,045	5.5
1964	148	625	4.2	186	1,350	7.3

Source: "Daily Digests" of various volumes of the *Congressional Record*.

ties are particularly important as secondary work for the member. Would this be likely to change with a longer term? Davidson et al. do not think so:

> . . . there is no assurance that longer terms would lighten these burdens perceptibly. Constituency service and communications are not, by and large, regulated by the proximity of elections. There is no reason to think that Senators have proportionately less constituency work because they enjoy 6-year rather than 2-year terms. . . . The essential point . . . is that a very large portion of constituency-related tasks are not bound up in the frequency of elections.[5]

What would the member do with the extra time, if it materialized, of the longer term? The assumption of the long-termers is,

5. U. S. Cong., House, Committee on the Judiciary, Subcommittee No. 5, "Congressional Tenure of Office," 89 Cong., 1 and 2 sess. (1965–66), p. 297.

TABLE 17

Major Time-Consuming Activities of Members
of the House of Representatives

Type of activity	Major time-consuming activity	Important as secondary activity
Legislation, committee work	77%	20%
Casework, "errands" for constituents	16	58
Publicity, communication with district	3	38
Campaigning	3	14
Intra-House politics	1	10
Washington social life	0	4
	100%	144%ª

Source: U. S. Congress, Committee on Judiciary, Subcommittee No. 5, *Hearings*, "Congressional Tenure of Office," 89 Cong., 1 and 2 sess. (1965–66), p. 296.

ª The sum of the percentages of secondary activities exceeds 100 percent because a number of members mentioned more than one such activitiy.

of course, that he would work on public problems so as to become a better legislator. The members discussed this question in round tables:

CONGRESSMAN A: I think it would not affect it because the nature of a person [determines whether he] is going to be a student and be responsible and show energy and initiative. It will be the same whether he is in for four years or two years. You [Congressman C] wouldn't act any differently in a four-year term.

CONGRESSMAN B: He would get lazier and he knows it. We all would. We would get lazier.

CONGRESSMAN C: I would not be doing the kind of thing that I think is the most fruitful in getting knowledge and that is building up this relationship with the constituency.

Other members were convinced that the additional time would be devoted to public problems and their solutions—that the demands created by the present system simply prevent adequate consideration of legislative problems. One member candidly remarked that he would "probably take trips and I am not sure the taxpayer ought to have to pay for that."

Several conclusions can be set forth as a result of analyzing the limited data available on this subject. First and foremost, how a member allocates his time depends on a number of variables aside from the length of his term. Particularly important is his view of the job. Constituency-oriented members will probably not change the manner in which they use their time if given a longer term unless they change their interpretation of their responsibilities as well. "Constant campaigner" types will probably continue with the same sorts of activities as before. Second, it does appear that the House could arrange its business so as to use time more efficiently. They stretch their days in session over a long period of time and the average time in session on any one day is rather low. It is interesting to note that the Joint Committee on the Organization of Congress made recommendations on this problem.[6] Third, members now apparently spend most of their time on legislation; what the increment would be if there were a four-year term is almost impossible to determine.

The Staff Problem

Closely related to the problem of how the member allocates his time is how staff time is allocated. There are three major staff activities: constituency service (usually called "case work"), campaign work, and legislative work. Obviously, these activities overlap and thus it is difficult to provide precise definition of what each includes. In his study of congressional staffs, Warren H. Butler does offer some general descriptions of the service and legislative functions which are serviceable, however:

The service function encompasses all of the myriad demands for assistance and requests for information from private citizens and public officials that flow into the Member's office from the State or district every day. The legislative function includes obtaining the views of constituents and expressing the Member's own as an elected representative, the initiation of ideas within the legislative process,

6. See U. S. Cong., Senate, Joint Committee on the Organization of Congress, "Organization of Congress," 89 Cong., 2 sess. (1966), Report No. 1414, p. 55.

the evaluation of legislative proposals, and the review of the consequences as well as the administration of the laws.[7]

Campaign work would include those activities which are more directly related to the reelection of the member: getting nominating petitions, speechwriting for campaigns, scheduling campaign time, making arrangements in the district for campaign activities, sending out campaign literature, organizing, etc.

The member has a number of staff services at his disposal. For constituency-service work, he can rely on his own personal staff (which will vary from three to a maximum of eleven, with most at six or seven), the Legislative Reference Service, the bureaucracy, and, to a lesser extent, standing committee staffs. For campaign work he has to rely almost exclusively on his own staff, and party committee staffs, though he may get some indirect assistance from other staffs. For legislative work, he can rely on his staff, standing committee staffs (though there are problems, particularly for the minority, in getting assistance from staff who are appointed by senior members), the Legislative Reference Service, and the Legislative Counsel.[8]

Though there are a number of factors which are important in determining staff use (principally constituency characteristics and the member's view of his job),[9] all staffs spend most of their time on constituency-related problems. Campaign work and legislative work vary considerably office-to-office but the case load is high in practically every office. All of the round table participants shared this conclusion. Some of their comments were:

The principal job of the staff is to handle the mail and to answer these inquiries. . . . Obviously you can't sit in committee all morning and be on the floor all afternoon and answer 100 letters a day. Somebody has to be back there tending to all of that. I think that is the real duty of a staff. If it does a job right, you get reelected.

---

7. Warren H. Butler, "Administering Congress: The Role of the Staff," *Public Administration Review*, Vol. 26 (March, 1966), p. 3. See also Kenneth T. Kofmehl, *Professional Staffs of Congress* (Purdue University Press, 1962). Unfortunately there is only a very limited amount of information in Kofmehl about personal staffs.

8. *Ibid.*, pp. 4–5.

9. As Butler notes in discussing staff use, "Most important . . . is the Member's own personality and his own readings of the priorities and responsibilities associated with his position." *Ibid.*, p. 4.

————

I have one person who does legislative research work part of the time and I have six people that I call my communications link with my constituency.

————

My office is almost 100 percent oriented to doing things that will please constituents, so they will vote for me. And frankly, if you give me twice the staff, they would all be doing the same thing in my district, and in my office.

————

I have eleven people on my staff, and I will agree that the majority of those eleven people are devoted to doing things and listening to problems, and then contacting the departments and working those problems out. I have two people on my staff who never basically contact the public. . . . their job primarily is to analyze legislation, and keep me informed as best as possible with my committee work.

————

Most of the work of my staff is devoted to running the errands, contacting the departments, sending out literature, answering inquiries. A minimum of their time is spent on legislative work. This is dead wrong.

As the last quotation indicates, some members denigrate the value of casework—they do not consider that it is a proper function of a representative. Others take pride in the amount of this type of work which they and their staff can handle. And far from disapproving of these activities, some staff personnel consider the work essential to the representative process (perhaps in part because it is their job—what they were hired to do). One staff aide described such an operation:

As our office is run, there is a certain plateau of campaign operation throughout the two-year period. We hold weekly office hours in our district office, which are announced in regularly scheduled newsletters. . . . Those office hours are anticipated and people are aware, and we have 100 to 150 people per day over a three-day period. Last year he [the congressman] went to [the district] 56 times, at his own expense most of the time, and I went 19 times. What we did primarily for a good Thursday and Friday . . . or Friday and Saturday . . . was to see warm body problems, as we call them. These are people who come [to] us for assistance in any one of the agencies. We established, about four years ago, an appellate structure whereby the [district] staff, which is equally as large as our Washington staff, tries to handle the problem, where the local agency is involved, with the local agency, and if that doesn't work, we get it, to try it on the Washington level of the same agency.

Unquestionably constituency demands would continue even if House members were given a four-year term. Senate staffs are also kept fully occupied with the flood of constituency-related problems.[10] The longer term would presumably have two effects. First, long-term proponents argue that there would be a reduction in the number of constituency-related matters which are picked up at campaign time. Both members and staff agreed that House members tend to get more casework simply because they are forced by biennial elections to go home often:

CONGRESSMAN A: . . . we generate activity by going home all the time.
CONGRESSMAN B: Do your Senators go home every weekend?
CONGRESSMAN A: No. If we were somewhat removed, as the Senators are, we wouldn't generate as much correspondence and questioning. If you go home and go to dinner, by the time you walk from the head table to the rear door, five people will come up to you. "Will you take care of this? It is all written out, and you will understand it tomorrow." You have picked up five matters in that evening.
CONGRESSMAN B: I would hate like the devil not to pick up five matters.
CONGRESSMAN A: So would I. But it generates work.

Staff aides discussed this process from their point of view:

Sometimes it is necessary to be as close to the guy as possible. He is throwing stuff out of a car window and you are picking up the stuff from the sidewalk. At eleven o'clock at night, when he is going home to sleep, you are going back to the office to unscramble his coffee-spilled notes, and so forth. You all have had that.

———

I spend seven or eight hours, maybe more, on this business [which results from] picking up these things out of the pockets of the congressmen and out of mine. I pick them up and go back at night [to sort them out], sometimes I get up at six o'clock the next morning.

10. Many, of course, have suggested an "ombudsman" to relieve the members of these tasks. See H. Douglas Price, "The Electoral Arena," in David B. Truman (ed.), *The Congress and America's Future* (Prentice-Hall, 1965), pp. 48–49, and the *Hearings* of the Joint Committee on the Organization of the Congress.

The second effect of eliminating one election, it is argued, would be to reduce the amount of staff time directly devoted to campaign activities. How much time is currently spent on campaign activities? Once again, the answer must be, "It all depends." Significant differences in the campaign activities of top staff aides were apparent in the Brookings round table discussions. Some aides are campaign managers and are very much preoccupied with that activity during an election year:

> I have run my boss's campaign since 1954, as I suppose ——— has. . . . I am the political man in my office, mainly because my boss doesn't particularly care for it. . . . I take care of the machines. We spend about eight weeks in a campaign at which time I go out and run the campaign, not as a campaign manager, but through other people.

> ———

> I guess I am legislative assistant and campaign manager. I work for a member who runs about . . . 60 percent in the final election. . . . Like ——— says, I am the campaign manager. I contract for the billboards and the radio time and the television time and bumper stickers and all that. . . . In the last six months before the final election, then I would say I average out 50 percent [on campaign activities].

These political campaign activities may well include fundraising:

> I can raise as much money as he can raise, because I have more time to do it, and I am not as concerned with answering to the constituency as he is, so my mind is a little freer.

As noted earlier, there is an ethical question involved in using staff in this way. Apparently it depends in part on the constituency as to whether such practices cause difficulty for the member. The following exchange between two House members is illustrative.

> CONGRESSMAN A: One of my staff men is going back to the district and instead of doing a job in Washington he is going to be back there working for the next four or five months until the election takes place.
> CONGRESSMAN B: Are you going to report his expenses?
> CONGRESSMAN A: I am engaging more staff out in the district and not in my congressional office, because it is an election year. If we didn't have that election, that staff would be here performing duties which are more closely identified with congressional legislative work than

with campaign activities. . . . I am sure that must be the general attitude in all congressional offices.

CONGRESSMAN B: No, sir.

CONGRESSMAN C: No, indeed.

CONGRESSMAN B: I don't send people back to campaign. That is dangerous business in my district. You can get criticized for it seriously. It can kill you.

Staff aides made similar observations in round table discussions. As one noted: "I never work on the campaign. [Laughter] How confidential is this meeting? . . . It hasn't happened to me personally but it has happened to senators' aides, other congressmen's aides, if they go back and campaign, they attack them for having their people back in the district."

Even standing committee staff may be drawn into the campaign—writing speeches, providing background material on legislation "that [the members] might have let go up to this time." How much committee staff time is involved and what is the effect? One staff member gave this opinion in the round table discussion:

It is significant enough, both . . . for the majority and . . . for the minority. I think it substantially impairs the assistance the committees get during the campaign in committee work. . . . In an election year there seems to be so much emphasis on winning that a congressman, although he might be reluctant, utilizes his staff for that purpose, whatever he can get.

Some congressional staff spend very little time on campaign activities. Either the district is safe, or the member prefers to handle campaigning on his own:

It depends on what kind of constituency you have. . . . If you work for a congressman who is lucky enough . . . to build up 75 percent majorities or 65 percent majorities, then you don't have these same pressures. . . . In our particular office . . . if you would take all of the staff hours in a given year and say how much of these staff hours are being spent on campaigns . . . , I suppose 10 to 15 percent would be all in our office that would be spent along these lines.

———

From a political standpoint, my member handles everything himself. We have no political organization. We have no full time campaign manager. We have no primary. . . . So I may spend, from the standpoint of what you might call regular political campaigning, perhaps a week or two in the district.

—————

I have not been in our congressional district in the seven years I have been here. . . . If you consider campaigning as what we cannot do under the frank, I do very little campaigning. . . . My boss runs it. He runs his own campaign.

In some cases these staff members whose members come from relatively safe districts may assist candidates in other campaigns —outside their districts—since they are not needed at home.

A strong case can be made that *some* members would gain additional staff time from their not having to campaign every two years. The question then becomes one of how they would use this staff time. More staff time could be allotted to constituency problems or to legislative matters or to both. The proponents of a longer term have in mind that the member would use any additional staff time gained by the four-year term for the legislative function, not for improved or increased constituency service. The staff deficiency at present is in the legislative area. As Charles L. Clapp observes:

Most House offices probably do not have anyone with important responsibilities in connection with legislation. In fact, the main deficiency in staffing may be the absence of a qualified legislative assistant who can do research for the congressman and help him perform his legislative role more efficiently.[11]

And as Butler indicates in his definition of staff functions, there are a number of legislative activities to occupy staff. Perhaps the most difficult of these is the initiation of ideas—the creativity which results in solutions to public problems. Can it be expected that members will employ additional staff time to assist them in their legislative work? That would depend entirely on the members—on how they define their job. The staff advantages of the long term will not make ineffective legislators effective. Two staff participants in the round tables explained:

I think in terms of legislation and serving the district, a good congressman can legislate and serve his district, whether he has a two- or

11. Clapp, *op. cit.,* p. 61. Butler also discusses this problem; *ibid.,* pp. 11–13.

four-year term. A bad and indifferent congressman will not serve his district and not concern himself with legislation, whether he has a two- or four-year term.

_____

Aren't you really saying . . . if you have a staff that is devoted to errands, that is because the boss wants to be devoted to errands? If you have one or two people that are devoted to legislation, it is because the boss wants it.

This is not to say, of course, that there are no beneficial effects of additional staff for members but that one cannot expect uniformly good results.

The short-term proponents do not accept the conclusion that constituency-service staff work and legislative staff work can be so neatly distinguished. As has been noted in Chapter II, many of them argue that legislation results from constituency contacts. Thus, when staff personnel are serving the constituency, they are discovering ideas for legislation.

It is very difficult to develop conclusions based on facts, when it comes to the argument over the legislative work of staff. There are no reliable data about the amount of staff time spent on legislative matters—only generalizations about the excessive amount of time spent on constituency service. Neither are there data on the amount of legislation which can be traced to the constituency-service activities of staff. On balance, it does seem that a longer term would provide additional staff time for some House members. Would that staff time be used creatively? Or, can the staff problem be solved in other ways? What constitutes "creative use" of staff? There are presently no objectively derived answers to these questions.

Summary

There are definite policy effects of the two-year term. The evidence indicates that mid-term elections can create real difficulties for the President—particularly a minority party President (e.g., Woodrow Wilson, 1918; and Dwight D. Eisenhower, 1954 and

1958). Most members must take time to campaign frequently and use valuable staff time on campaign activities. And there surely are controversial legislative measures which get postponed because of election year politics (though analysis of the extent to which Congress willingly goes on record regarding the presidential program does not support this conclusion). But there is much less agreement on the extent to which these are "adverse" effects than is true regarding electoral effects. Thus, there is considerable (though not conclusive) support in this chapter for a longer term for House members *if* one believes that the President should have a friendlier Congress, that members should not campaign as often as they do now, that more staff time should be diverted to other purposes than constituency service, and that all controversial matters should receive attention in election years. If one has other preferences, however, as many congressmen do, then the evidence presented in this chapter will not be very convincing.

CHAPTER
FIVE

SOLVING THE PROBLEM
OF THE TWO-YEAR TERM

When they set the term of the House at two years, the founding fathers took other actions which made it unlikely that this aspect of the Constitution could easily be changed. For example: they made it difficult to amend the Constitution, they made Congress responsible for reforming itself, and they articulated a persuasive rationale for the two-year compromise, particularly in *The Federalist*. Thus, for any change to be made now in the length of term for House members, the strongest possible case would have to be presented. A strong case can be defined as one which permits some reasonably reliable prediction that the outcome of the change will benefit the membership, the institution, and the nation. Constitutional amendments are, after all, significant and infrequent events in the history of congressional action—an average of only one every twelve years, and only two of these, the 17th and 20th amendments, have had to do with congressional organization.

This study has attempted to evaluate the strength of the case for lengthening the term of House members. It is now appropriate to draw some of the threads together, in order to determine whether a change *should* be made. What are the *conditions* for

97

change? It seems logical that the reformer should be able to prove that there are *effects* of the two-year term which are deleterious to the representative process in the House and that his reform proposal will remove these effects. He should also be able to demonstrate that these effects are widespread, not isolated, and are perceived as deleterious by the members themselves. One of the conditions for change in a democratic system is agreement among a sizable portion of those affected, that reform is necessary. Further, the proponent of change should be able to demonstrate that there will be no offsetting negative effects of the longer term.

What are the effects of the two-year term? How widespread are these effects? Which, if any, are deleterious to the representative process in the House and can, therefore, be labeled "problems" of the two-year term? How much agreement is there among members about these "problems?" Are there ways short of lengthening the term which might solve problems which do exist? What is the likelihood that the problems of the two-year term will be solved by lengthening the term to four years? It is these questions which will now receive attention.

The Effects of the Two-Year Term

There are both electoral and policy effects of the two-year term on congressional behavior, most of which cannot be precisely measured. The principal electoral effect is the high dollar cost of campaigning. Despite the lack of reliable information on costs, it is clear that most members find it expensive to run for the House of Representatives every second year. Further, the mental, physical, and family costs of campaigning are very demanding for some members. The two-year term apparently does not, however, have the effect of attracting the unqualified and repelling the qualified, of causing instability in the House through rapid turnover of membership, or of encouraging issue-oriented campaigns.

Reformers have spotted a number of policy effects of the two-year term, which can be supported by evidence. First, the President's party usually suffers losses at the mid-term election and he will, therefore, have less support for his program in Congress. Second, frequent campaigning does take time from other activities. Indeed, a few members find it necessary to run twice and sometimes three times (if there is a runoff primary) in one year to retain their seat. Third, House members' staffs tend to become very constituency-service oriented in their work and they, too, must divert some of their energies to campaigning. The result of frequent campaigning, it is argued, is a campaign-constituency orientation in the House of Representatives, particularly in election years, which has definite policy effects (though these cannot be measured with any degree of precision). It is also argued that controversial legislation is avoided during election years. While probably true in certain cases, it is difficult to demonstrate that this is a widespread phenomenon.

The Problems of the Two-Year Term

There is considerable disagreement about whether the effects mentioned above can be classified as "problems"—that is, as having adverse effects on the representative process. One man's problem may be another man's principle. Based on the round table discussions, the hearings, and other sources of opinion, there seems to be general agreement that the high cost of campaigning is a definite problem for most members. Concern is also generally expressed about the workload of members and their staffs—in part as a result of the two-year term. Thus, there *is* agreement about the existence of problems which result, in some measure, from the short term.

There is, however, basic disagreement between proponents and opponents of the long term, on the extent to which other effects of the two-year term can be labeled "problems." In particular, the proponents view the mid-term election as a problem, in that it normally results in a reduced margin for the President's party in Congress and therefore less support for his program. Opponents claim, however, that this is one of the strengths of the system. The voters should be given a chance to express themselves every two years. A four-year term, concurrent with the President, may be more convenient for House members and for the President, but not for the voters. Proponents also see frequent campaigning as a problem since it takes time away from a member's legislative responsibilities. Opponents disagree that this is a problem, since they argue that campaigning forces the representative to maintain contact with his constituency, and that contact should form the basis of legislative behavior.

What Is the Best Solution?

Basic disagreement about what the problems are makes it difficult to determine solutions. There are three leading solutions to the "problem of the two-year term." If the problem is eventually identified as one of providing a greater guarantee of *support* for the President, and more *time* for the member to fulfill his legislative responsibilities, then the four-year term concurrent with the President appears to be a perfectly reasonable solution—indeed, the only type of term change which makes sense. If most members eventually agree that frequent elections simply *cost* too much and do not allow the member enough *time* to fulfill his legislative responsibilities, but that voters ought to be given a chance every two years to express themselves, then the staggered four-year term is a possibility, if the formidable technical problems can be worked out satisfactorily (an unlikely prospect). If most members eventually agree that the problem of the two-year term is principally an administrative or management problem in the House itself, then the length of term does not have to be changed at all. The problem can be solved in other ways.

It may now be appropriate to introduce the author's judgment about a solution. After studying the arguments and evaluating the relatively limited amount of data available, I have concluded that no length-of-term change should be made at this time.

In the first place, the adverse effects of the two-year term are by no means as obvious as the long-term proponents claim. As has been noted, some effects cannot be demonstrated to exist to any great extent, others are extremely difficult to prove with existing data, and some which do clearly exist are not uniformly relevant for all members (or even a large majority of members).

Second, where it is possible to demonstrate that there are effects from the two-year term, not all members (or students of Congress) would agree that the effects are adverse to the goals of the House of Representatives. (This is particularly true of policy effects.) There always have been, and will continue to be, different interpretations of how one should represent in Congress.

Third, there are major problems, both technical and substantive, in the compromise proposal which has the most support; the staggered-term proposal. If a change is to be made eventually, the staggered-term compromise is not a reasonable alternative. Either the concurrent-term proposal should be adopted, or the system should remain as it is.

There are other reasons for not changing the length of term, most importantly the definite advantages of the system as it exists. In an age in which an increasingly complex society requires an elaborate governmental structure to serve the public, there is something to be said for maintaining frequent contact between the people and their government. A four-year term may be more convenient for the President and the members themselves, but not for the voters. Any political system may be measured by the distance between the public and its decision-makers. Americans have rather consistently favored the idea that it is better to have less distance, rather than more, between these two. As government expands to meet the demands of modern society, the public, more than ever, should have someone with whom they can communicate. It is a fact, of course, that most citizens do not communicate with their congressmen. But it is not necessary for a large number of constituents to communicate with their representatives in order to justify the two-year term. The potential is there and, further, because of the short term the member does make an effort to communicate with his constituents and attend to their needs—both legitimate functions in government.

It can be argued, therefore, that, far from being outdated, it is more important now than ever before that the two-year term for congressmen be retained. I accept that argument, pending more convincing evidence to the contrary from the proponents of change.

Some Pragmatic Solutions

The fact remains that certain effects which can be demonstrated to exist are generally accepted as being "adverse effects." Should any action be taken to remedy these effects? There are some steps which can be taken that do not require amending the Constitution. The most obvious is new legislation on congressional campaign expenses. Realistic limitations on spending, better reporting, some enforcement of the law, encouragement, or incentives to contribute to political parties—these are changes which are overdue and would help to curb the rising spiral of campaign costs. There appears to be some likelihood that some changes in the present law will eventually pass.[1] It is within the power of Congress to help itself in this area, without a constitutional amendment. *If no action is taken, one is justified in questioning whether congressmen really are as concerned about this problem of the two-year term as they say they are.*

If it were legally possible to shorten the campaign, so that members would not feel compelled to campaign full time during the election year, this could relieve one of the problems of the two-year term. A difficulty in doing this is that the states set the nominating procedure and the date on which nominations will take place. It would be possible, however, for Congress to establish the direct primary as the nominating method for all candidates and set a date for all congressional primaries which is relatively close (perhaps in early October) to the first Tuesday after the first Monday in November. If this were combined with very stringent and enforceable campaign finance legislation which prohibited expenditures in the primary and general elections be-

1. President Johnson proposed campaign financing reform in his 1966 State of the Union message. As of this writing, some hearings had been held in the House, and the Senate had reported a watered-down bill, which did not include many of the President's requests.

fore a certain date, limited the amount of money to be spent in both elections, and encouraged contributions through tax incentives, the result might be, over a period of time, that members would spend less time campaigning. The problems involved in shortening the campaign and reducing costs are formidable, but are solvable short of amending the Constitution. A first step would be to appoint a special subcommittee with a well-trained research staff to study these problems and develop imaginative solutions.

Other changes which would assist in solving the problems of the two-year term have been suggested by the Joint Committee on the Organization of Congress. The problem for members in scheduling their time would be resolved to a certain extent if Congress were to schedule its business more efficiently. The Joint Committee suggests scheduling committee and floor business on a five-day work week instead of a three- or four-, requiring a majority roll call in each house to extend sessions beyond July 31, and providing for no session at all in August (except in time of war).[2] Certainly, as the Joint Committee report points out, a member's workload would not be reduced by these changes but the session would not be so "chopped up." Presumably, individual members would be able to fulfill their many functions more efficiently and perhaps even be able to find time to "contemplate" (whatever that may mean).

The Joint Committee also recommends increased standing committee staff, creating the position of legislative assistant for each member, and increasing the transportation allowances for members and their staffs.[3] The first two, in particular, would assist members in fulfilling their legislative responsibilities if in fact the staff is used for the purposes for which it was created.

These are changes which can be made to remedy some generally recognized adverse effects of the two-year term. But as with all reform of Congress, a great deal depends on the members' analysis of the effect of changes, as well as the effect of the status quo. House leaders and senior members, in particular, may be

2. U. S. Cong., Joint Committee on the Organization of the Congress, "Organization of Congress," Report No. 1414, 89 Cong., 2 sess. (1966), pp. 55–56.

3. *Ibid.*, pp. 21–23, 36–39.

expected to be overcautious in granting their support for procedural and structural changes. As Richard F. Fenno, Jr., points out, there are two basic problems of organization which the House must solve—that of establishing a decision-making structure and that of holding the decision-making structure together.[4] Leaders will assess reforms in terms of these problems. They are unlikely to press for changes if the existing internal distribution of influence in the House will be seriously unbalanced, or if there is some doubt about the matter. The whole thrust of this study suggests that there is considerable doubt about the effect of lengthening the term, on the organizational problems of the House. Reform will come only when the leadership and a large majority of members are assured that the changes will benefit the House in achieving its goals without threatening the existing order of things. To date, the proponents of change have not presented their case convincingly enough to assure the membership that a four-year term meets these requirements.

Prospects for a Constitutional Amendment

The House has made many changes in recent years to alleviate the problem of the two-year term without changing the length of term. Increases in staff, transportation allowances, increases in salary, more office space, and the like are all changes of this type. What is the likelihood that the House will now add to these a lengthened term for members? As indicated in Chapter II, most of the polls among members of Congress which were taken before 1966 indicated considerable support for the four-year term. Representative Chelf reported that 70 percent of his sample favored the staggered-term proposal. Davidson and his colleagues reported that 68 percent of their sample favored the concurrent-term proposal—44 percent being "strongly for" running with the President. Despite this apparently broad support for some kind

4. Richard F. Fenno, Jr., "The Internal Distribution of Influence: The House," in David Truman (ed.), *The Congress and America's Future* (Prentice-Hall, 1965), pp. 52–76.

of change, the President's proposal did not emerge from the House Committee on the Judiciary in 1966. Hearings were held in February and March, but no resolution was reported. Chairman Celler announced his strong opposition to any four-year-term proposal and lined up a number of witnesses who shared his beliefs. What looked like a possible constitutional amendment in January faded into one more futile attempt to change the length of House terms.

The Brookings 1966 Questionnaire

In late July, 1966, a mail questionnaire was sent to all House members, to get their views on the various proposals for changing the length of term and their opinions on the likelihood of any proposal succeeding in the 90th Congress. Apparently, no previous poll had asked the members to distinguish among the various four-year- and three-year-term proposals. The results of this mail questionnaire are quite different from the earlier polls reported in Chapter II. A total of 318 members (a return of 73.4 percent of the membership of the House at the time—433) returned the questionnaire, though not all members answered every item. The Republican return was higher than the Democratic—81 percent as compared to 68 percent. Members were asked to check whether they were "strongly for," "for," "neutral," "against," or "strongly against," the following:

A four-year term concurrent with the President,
A four-year term—all members elected in the off-year,
A four-year term—half of the members elected in the off-year, half with the President,
A three-year term, or
Keeping the two-year term.

Respondents did not have to identify themselves and most did not. Of those who returned the questionnaire, approximately one-half favored some sort of change in the length of term. They did not all agree on what form it should take, however, and those who favored one proposal were often against other proposals.

TABLE 18

House Members' Attitudes on Length-of-Term Proposals

Attitude	Proposal				
	Four-year term concurrent with President's term	Four-year term elected in off-year	Four-year term with staggered elections	Three-year term	No change
Strong approval	8.9	8.7	21.5	2.5	32.6
Approval	6.4	15.1	25.2	12.0	28.8
Subtotal	15.3	23.8	46.7	14.5	61.4
Neutrality	6.8	11.0	6.5	23.5	13.7
Disapproval	31.5	38.1	25.2	35.5	16.7
Strong disapproval	46.5	27.1	21.6	26.5	8.2
Subtotal	77.9	65.2	46.8	62.0	24.9
Total	100.0	100.0	100.0	100.0	100.0
NUMBER OF RESPONDENTS	(235)	(218)	(246)	(200)	(233)

Source: Questionnaire mailed to all House members, July 22, 1966.

Thus, for example, of the 160 who favored some change, 70 of those who were for either the staggered-term proposal, the off-year proposal, or the three-year term, were *against* the concurrent-term proposal. This division of opinion among proponents of some change in the length of term would make it very difficult to construct the necessary two-thirds majority for a constitutional amendment.

Table 18 presents the overall results of the questionnaire. None of the proposals for change was supported by even a simple majority of the sample, let alone a two-thirds majority. *Least* popular was the President's proposal for four-year terms, concurrent with his term. Nearly 80 percent of those responding on this proposal were opposed and almost 50 percent were strongly opposed. The off-year proposal was only slightly more popular, and the three-year term received very little support. The only proposed change to receive sizable support was the staggered-term proposal. Support and opposition were equally divided. Clearly, this is the only proposal which presently has any chance of passing the House and, given the requirement of a two-thirds majority, its chances must be rated as very slight. Further, as noted in Chapter II, there are complicated technical problems in developing a workable plan.

The present two-year term, on the other hand, appears to be popular with the members. Even some of those who favored the staggered- or off-year proposals preferred the two-year term to the concurrent-term proposal. Certainly, the overall conclusion from Table 18 is that, as of 1966, there was very little enthusiasm for a change.

Perhaps the sample is biased; that those who oppose term changes returned the questionnaire and those who are in favor did not. Even if this were so, there is enough opposition indicated in the results to cast grave doubts about the basis of support for change. Table 19 shows those opposed to the various proposals *as a percentage of the total House membership.* Since one-third plus one of the House can defeat a constitutional amendment, there are more than enough members opposed to the President's proposal in the sample alone to defeat it, and nearly enough opposed to the off-year proposal to defeat it. The number opposed

TABLE 19

Members Opposed to Various Term Change Proposals
as a Percentage of the Total Membership
of the House, 1966

Proposal	Number opposed[a]	*Percentage of the House*
Four-year term concurrent with President's term	183	*42.1%*
Four-year term elected in off-year	142	*32.6*
Four-year term with staggered elections	115	*26.4*
Three-year term	124	*28.5*

Source: Mail questionnaire.
[a] Those who indicated that they were "against" or "strongly against" the proposal.

to the staggered-term and three-year-term proposals in the sample is not enough to defeat an amendment but the percentages are still quite high. Since the three-year-term proposal received so little support (only 14.5 percent of the sample, and 6.7 percent of the House) it cannot be taken as a serious proposal.

As noted before, the question becomes whether there is enough support for the staggered-term proposal. Those in the sample who opposed it constitute 26.4 percent of the whole House. In addition, there were 29 members in the sample who indicated that they were either "strongly for" or "for" keeping the two-year term but did not indicate their attitudes toward the various proposals. If it is assumed that these 29 were opposed to any term changes (that is, they considered it superfluous to check that they were against the other proposals if they favored keeping the two-year term), then 144 members, 33.1 percent, oppose the staggered-term proposal.

There is another way to make the same point. A total of 140 members indicated in the poll that they favored keeping the two-year term. That figure is only five shy of the necessary one-third plus one of the House necessary to defeat a constitutional amendment.

There are significant differences between the two parties in their responses. The Republicans were generally opposed to all changes, and most opposed to the President's proposal (see Table 20). No Republican in the sample favored the concurrent-term plan. No doubt the fact that so many Republicans were defeated in normally Republican districts in the 1964 election was an important factor in their attitudes. They could not be expected to favor eliminating the 1966 election when it represented an opportunity to regain control of these seats. (Of course, no amendment would go into effect so soon, but many Republicans were likely influenced in their thinking by the immediate situation.) The only proposal to receive any substantial Republican backing was the staggered-term plan.

The Democrats showed more support for all proposals (see Table 20), but only the staggered-term plan received support of a majority of those responding. The President's concurrent-term proposal found favor with only one-fourth of those responding.

House members were also asked to state their opinions on the prospects in the 90th Congress of getting a change in the length of term. As is indicated in Table 21, members were not sanguine about the possibility of getting a four-year term in the immediate future. Over 80 percent of those responding considered it unlikely or very unlikely that there would be action on the matter in the 90th Congress.[5] There were only minor differences between the parties, with the Democrats slightly more optimistic than the Republicans.

Given the fact that there is considerable support for a longer term posed against even greater support for keeping the two-year term, cannot we expect that a compromise will eventually be developed? The two-year term itself was the result of a compromise at the Constitutional Convention. There is no doubt that any lengthening of the term of House members would be the result of a compromise, if and when there is greater support for change than there is now. But the two situations are not really compa-

5. These findings are very close to those of Davidson, Kovenock, and O'Leary. Their sample showed: very likely, 1 percent; likely, 5 percent; 50–50, 17 percent; unlikely, 39 percent; and very unlikely, 38 percent. See *Congress in Crisis: Politics and Congressional Reform* (Wadsworth, 1966), Appendix B.

TABLE 20

Party Attitudes on Length-of-Term Proposals

Attitude	Proposal				
	Four-year term concurrent with President's term	Four-year term elected in off-year	Four-year term with staggered elections	Three-year term	No change
Democrats:					
Approval[a]	25.4%	28.3%	55.3%	17.9%	51.5%
Neutrality	9.9	12.6	7.9	25.9	15.4
Disapproval[b]	64.7	59.1	36.8	56.2	33.1
Total	100.0	100.0	100.0	100.0	100.0
NUMBER OF RESPONDENTS	(142)	(127)	(152)	(112)	(130)
Republicans:					
Approval[a]	0.0%	17.8%	32.6%	10.3%	73.0%
Neutrality	2.2	8.9	3.3	20.7	12.0
Disapproval[b]	97.8	73.3	64.1	69.0	15.0
Total	100.0	100.0	100.0	100.0	100.0
NUMBER OF RESPONDENTS	(92)	(90)	(92)	(87)	(100)

Source: Mail questionnaire.
a Includes "strong approval" as well as "approval."
b Includes "strong disapproval" as well as "disapproval."

TABLE 21

House Members' Opinion on Prospects for Length-of-Term Change in 90th Congress, by Party, 1966

	Number of respondents	Prospects for change (percent)				
		Very likely	Likely	50–50	Unlikely	Very unlikely
Total[a]	302	*1.0%*	*3.3%*	*14.6%*	*46.7%*	*34.4%*
Democrats	190	*1.1*	*4.7*	*17.4*	*46.8*	*30.0*
Republicans	108	*0.9*	*0.9*	*9.3*	*46.3*	*42.6*

Source: Mail questionnaire.
[a] Includes four respondents for whom the party was unknown.

rable. The two-year term is a fact now. It has existed for over 175 years as a major characteristic of the House of Representatives. It is not necessary now, as it was in 1787, for a number to be inserted in the Constitution—one is already there. Further, the framers made it more difficult to change the number than it was to set it at two in the beginning. The amending process today is a much more "public" process than was the constitution-writing process in 1787, and it requires larger majorities. Finally, the two-year term was one small part of a vast document offered for state ratification in 1787. But the change to a four-year term would have to be debated in and of itself. All attention would be focused on those three words in Article I, "every second year."

All of this is not to say, of course, that there will *never be* a four-year term for House members. A future Congress could well bring new members who favor a four-year term, new proposals which are more workable than those presently suggested, and a change in the attitude of the party leadership. Further, the fact that many senior congressmen were defeated in 1966 may convince other senior members to change their minds and support the longer term. What the results of the questionnaire do indicate is that the large measure of consensus which is necessary for passage of a constitutional amendment does not presently exist.

The number opposed to any change is impressive and those who favor some change cannot agree on the form it should take.

Summary Observations

One of the characteristics of democracy is that it is full of dilemmas that are constantly debated but never quite resolved. The founding fathers offered a number of solutions when they produced a Constitution, but though the existence of the document had immense practical significance in setting up a government, it did not close off debate on fundamental democratic issues. Where the Constitution is specific—as with the two-year term for House members—formal change can only occur through the amending process. And when serious proposals are offered to make such changes, these proposals become the foci of debate on the principles of democracy. Old dilemmas are revisited and found to be no more resolvable now than they were in 1787. The problem of the two-year term is one more problem of democracy. Honest, sincere, dedicated public servants are frustrated by elections "every second year" because they think that representation would be improved if they could be released somewhat from the pressure to be constituency-oriented in their work. Other equally honorable members draw their sustenance from constituency contact. They do not wish to be released.

It is also characteristic of this democracy that it is reluctant to change institutional arrangements until the debate has spent itself. In this sense, democratic government is conservative government. If a high degree of consensus on solutions to basically irresolvable dilemmas is a requirement for constitutional change, then change of that type will be infrequent. That does not mean that change cannot or does not occur. Democratic government, under certain emergency conditions, can act with great speed, and extra-constitutional developments of major significance can take place over a period of time. In fact, it is this adaptability which allows democrats to be so protective both of formal institutional arrangements and the process of full debate for altering them.

Thus, lengthening the term of office for House members will remain on the agenda of Congress because it poses a significant question about the representative process in this democracy. Perhaps one day a new compromise will be accepted, just as the two-year compromise was accepted on June 21, 1787. But that compromise will be no more successful than its predecessor in silencing debate on the fundamental question it seeks to answer: *What is the proper function of a representative in the House of Representatives, and how best may this function be performed?*

INDEX

Adams, Samuel, 3
Amendment. *See* Constitutional amendment
Ames, Fisher, 12, 13
Articles of Confederation, 3

Bailey, Stephen K., 30, 30n
Bankhead, William B., 18n
Barber, James D., 45, 46n
Bayh, Birch, 24
Brookings questionnaire, 105–11
Brookings round table discussion, 34, 46–47, 55
Burnett, Edmund C., 3, 3n
Burns, James M., 21n, 30, 30n
Butler, David E., 49n, 94n
Butler, Warren H., 89n

Campaign expenses: actual versus reported, 55–56; difficulty in defining, 57; district differences in, 57–58; effect of candidate opposition on, 58; effect of newspaper support on, 59–60; effect of two-year term on, 21, 52–61; financing reforms for, 102; in Great Britain, 50; increase in, 26, 37–38; for incumbents and challenger, 60–61; new legislation for, 102–04; party help versus personal cost for, 59; raising money for, 57; in time consumed, 61–64; under four-year term, 27
Campaigning: contact with constituency during, 65–66; by freshmen congressmen, 69; quality of representation and, 63–64; reduction of time for, 102–03; value of, 63

Campbell, Angus, 73n
Casework. *See* Constituency service
Celler, Emanuel, 35, 40, 41, 104
Checks and balances, 12; under concurrent four-year term, 31, 38–39
Chelf, Frank, 22, 23, 24, 27, 31, 41, 42, 42n, 104
Clapp, Charles L., 28n, 53n, 94, 94n
Clark, Joseph S., 21n
Cochran, William B., 17
Committee on Detail, of Constitutional Convention of 1787, 6
Committee on Elections (House), 17
Committee of the Whole, of Constitutional Convention of 1787, 5, 7
Concurrent four-year term, 14, 22, 25, 30, 35; attitude of House members toward, 106–07; checks and balances and, 31, 38; to enhance prestige of Congress, 29; party attitude toward, 108–11; percentage of congressmen supporting, 104; as solution to problems of two-year term, 101; support of political scientists for, 30; support for President's program under, 78. *See also* Four-year term for House members
Congress: activity on four-year term in 79th, 18; House members' opinion on length of term change in 90th, 111; occupational background of members of 89th, 50; proposed improvement for scheduling business of, 103; reforms of 1945–46, 20; support for President's program, 73–78; three-